For Lilly

For Lilly...
on Her
60th
Birthday

The Merry Blacksmith Press • 2014

For Lilly… on Her 60th Birthday

For information, address:

The Merry Blacksmith Press
70 Lenox Ave.
West Warwick, RI 02893

merryblacksmith.com

Published in the USA by The Merry Blacksmith Press

ISBN— 978-1-49938-849-7
1-49938-849-7

Mom,

I was going to spend pages and pages talking about what a great mother you are. I was going to talk about how you successfully raised a daughter by yourself, while working full time. About how you defied all the odds and stereotypes, and ensured that I had love, stability, and didn't want for anything. How you worked tirelessly to make sure that I knew that I was special and important, and how you never made me feel like it was an effort to make me feel that way. How you made sure that I grew up knowing how to practice kindness and care about other people and the world around me. How because of the unconditional love you gave me, I grew up knowing how to love. That because of your example, I grew up into an adult who knows how to practice compassion,and how to practice (*sometimes!*) patience. That I was able to learn from your own examples of perseverance how to reach my own goals and achieve greatness. How you ignored everyone who said that you couldn't do it and did it, no matter what "it" was. I was going to talk about all this and more. Because you truly are my hero. I don't know how you did it all, but I am certainly glad that you did!

I was going to spend hours talking about all of that, and more. And then I realized I could say all of that in one sentence. I am who I am because you are who you are. And there is nothing better than who you are.

Thank you. For everything you've done, and everything you continue to do.

Love,

Margaret

PS: John thinks you are pretty amazing as well.
    He thanks you, too.

I sustain myself with the love of family.

– Maya Angelou

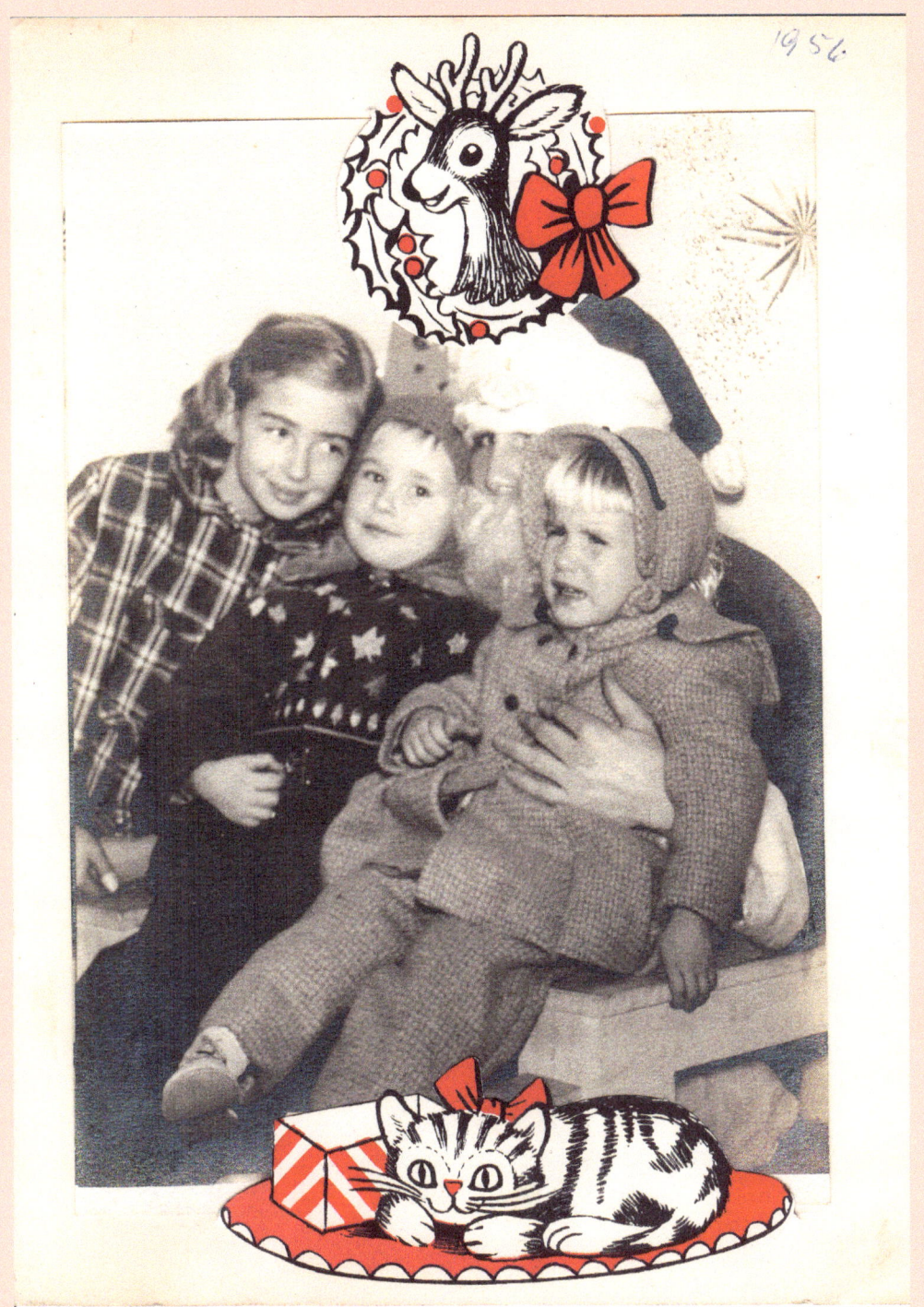

1956

1

Families are the compass that guides us. They are the inspiration to reach great heights, and our comfort when we occasionally falter.

– Brad Henry

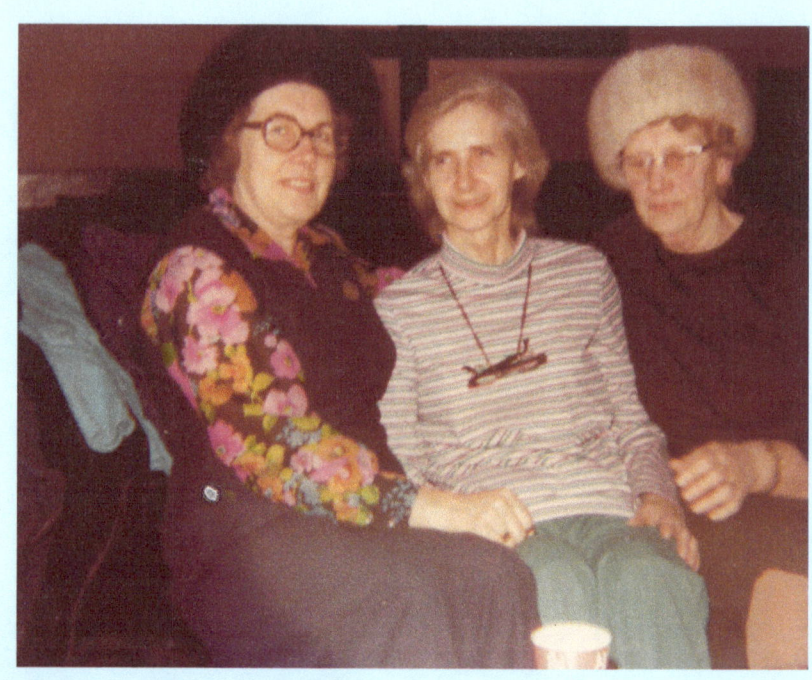

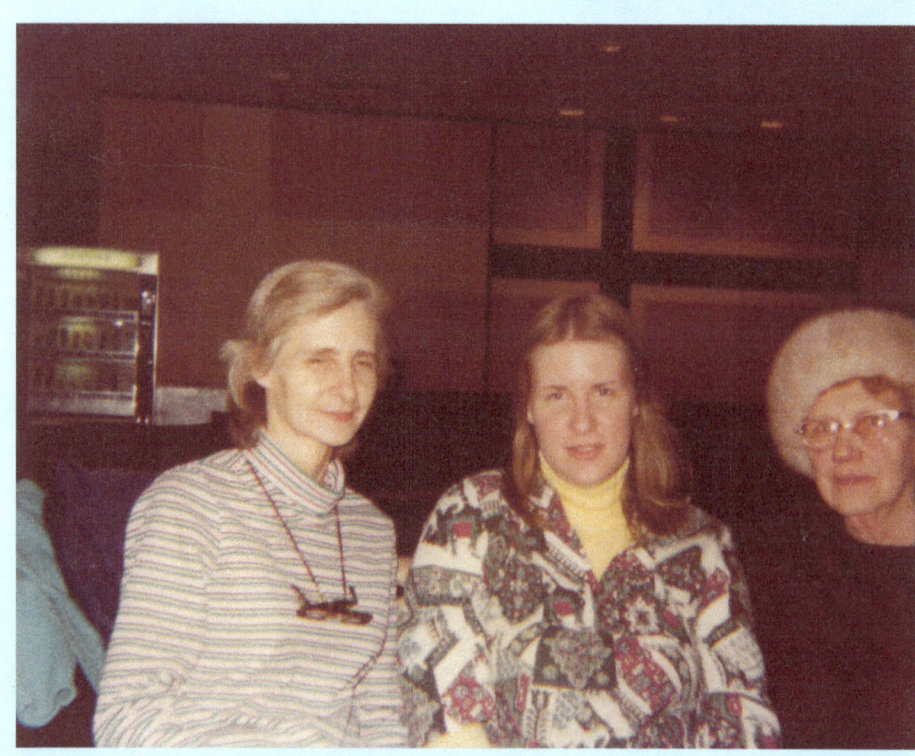

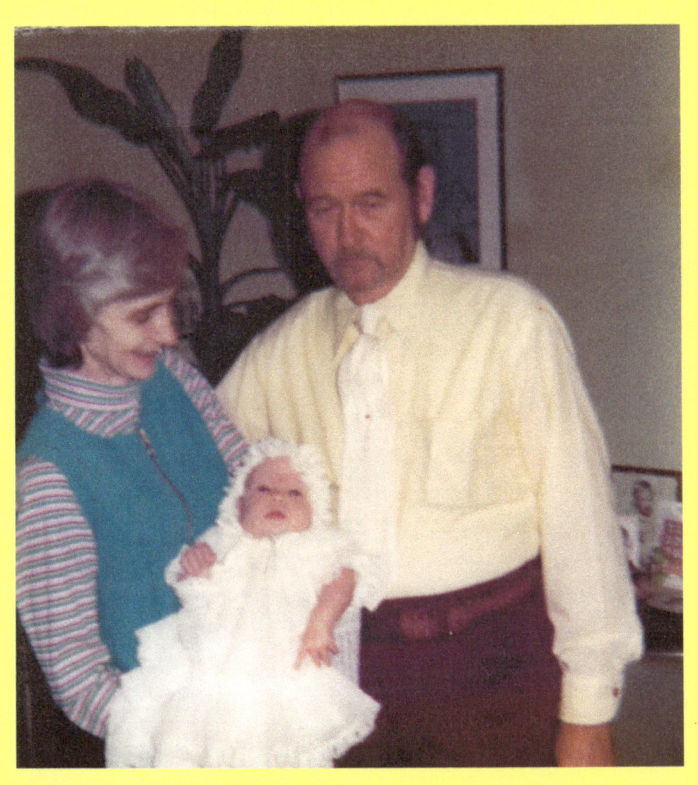

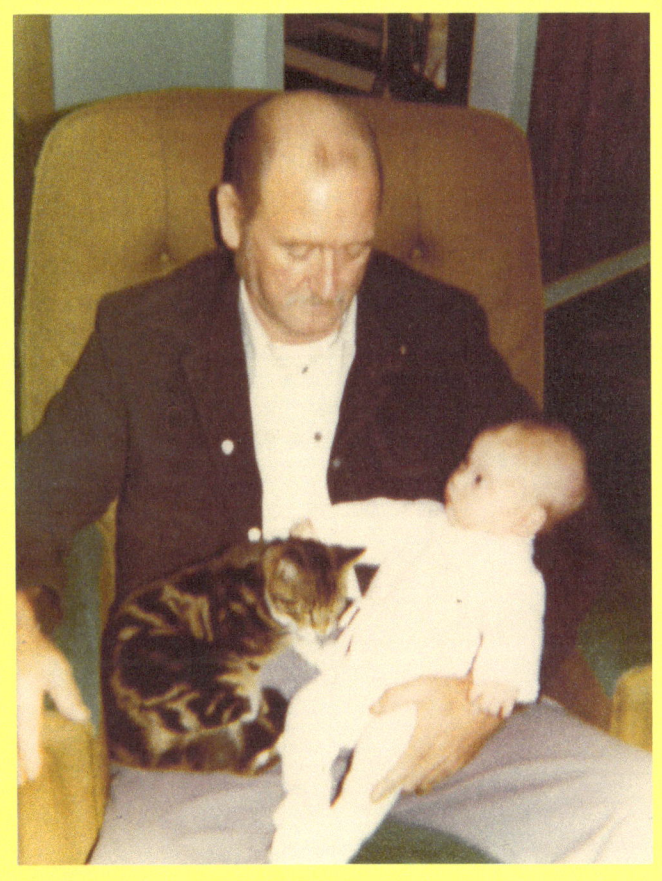

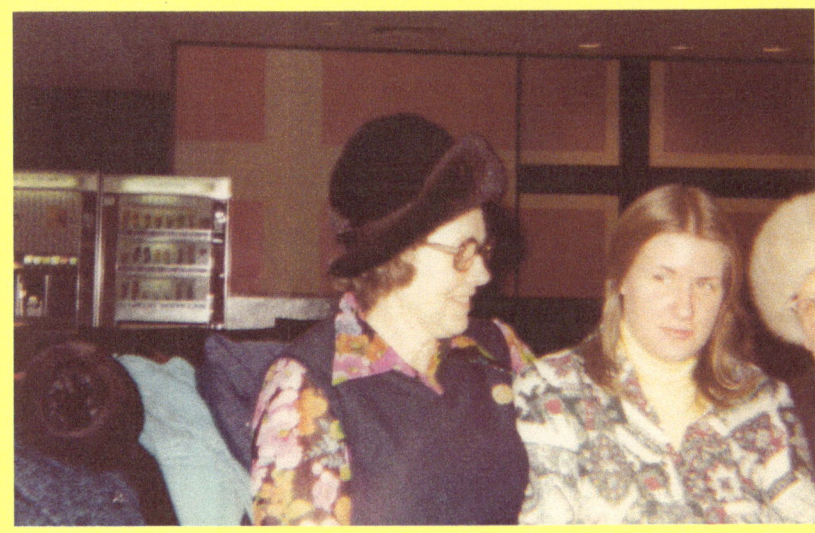

A family is a place where minds come in contact with one another.

– Buddha

3

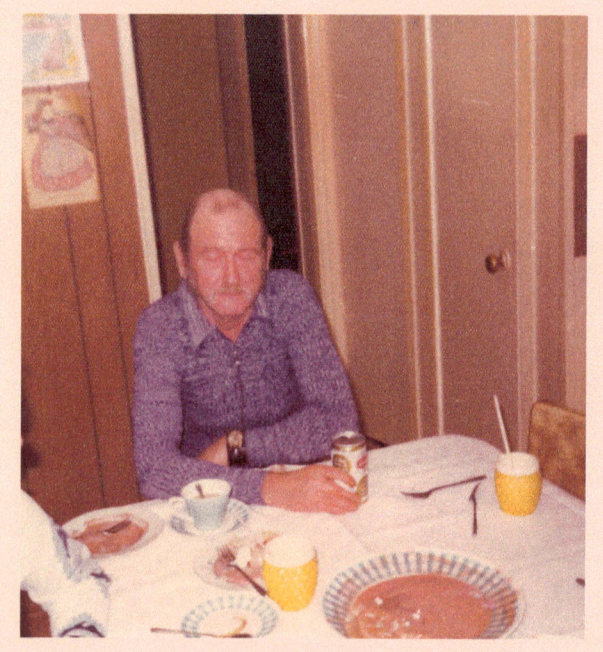

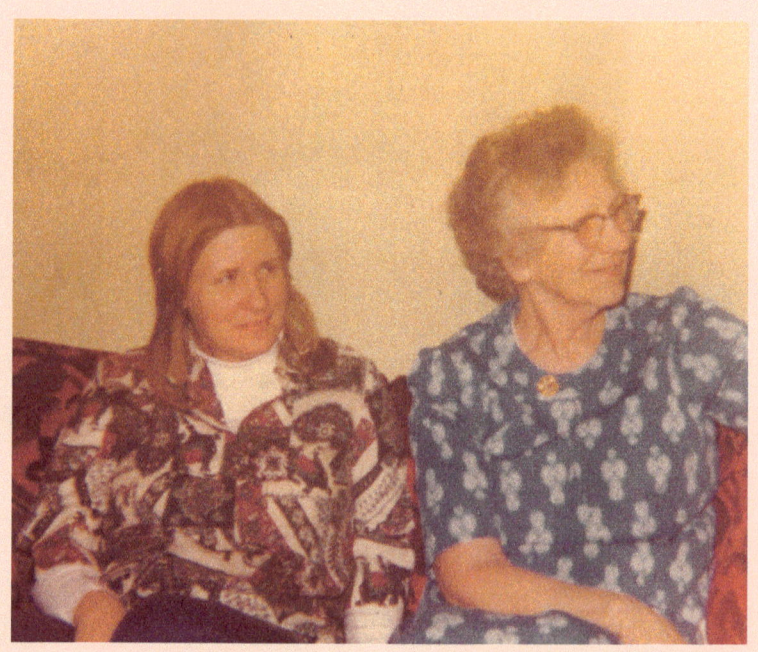

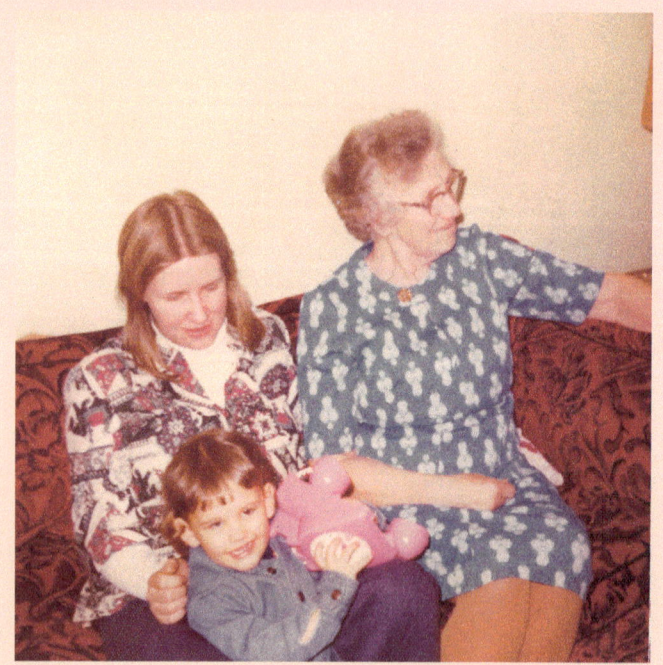

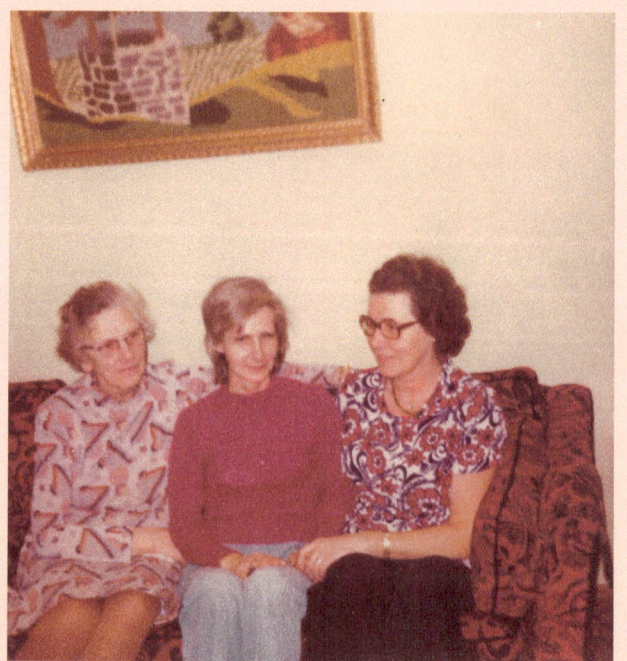

4

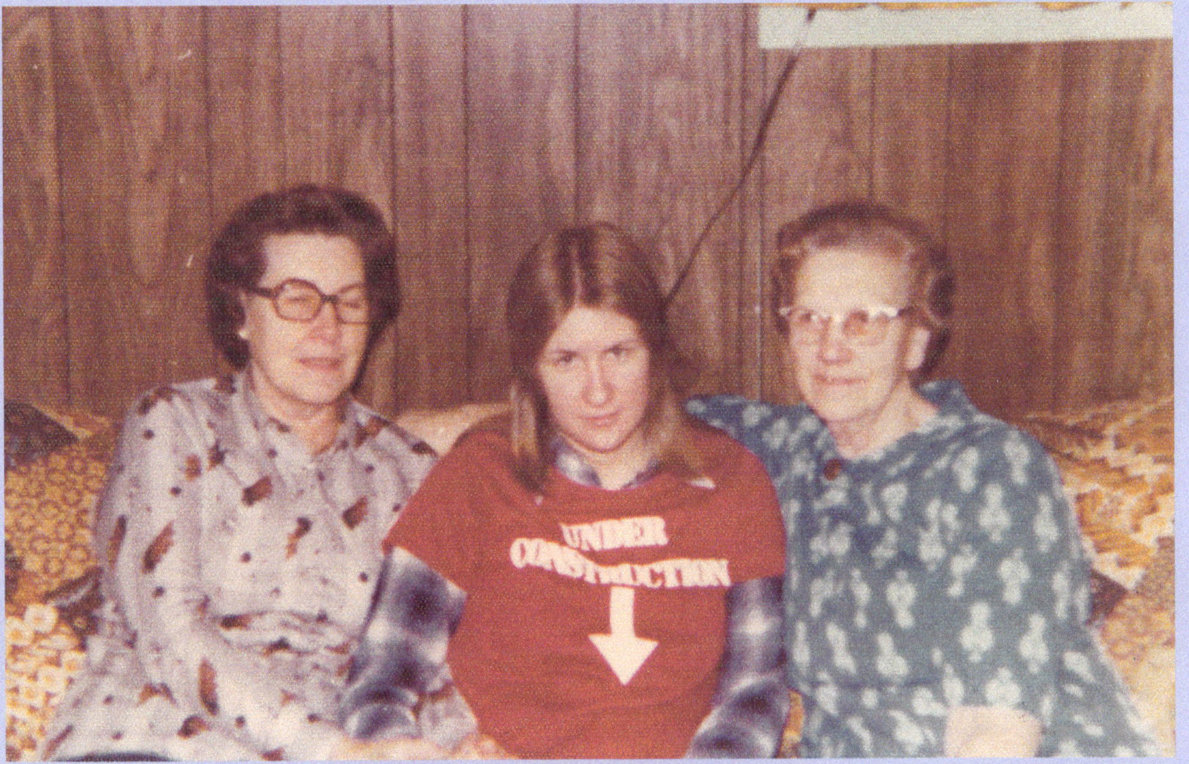

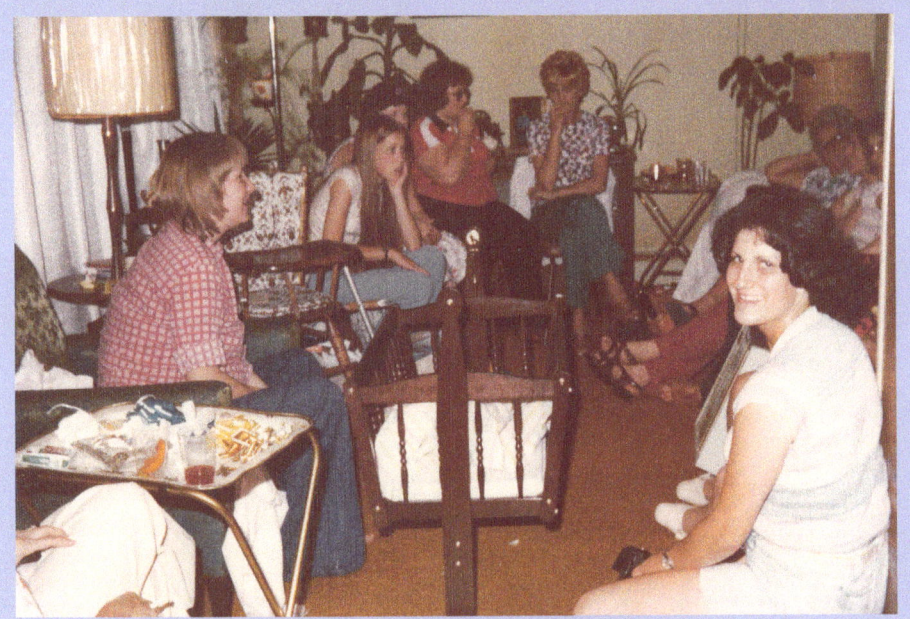

We must take care of our families wherever we find them.

– Elizabeth Gilbert

5

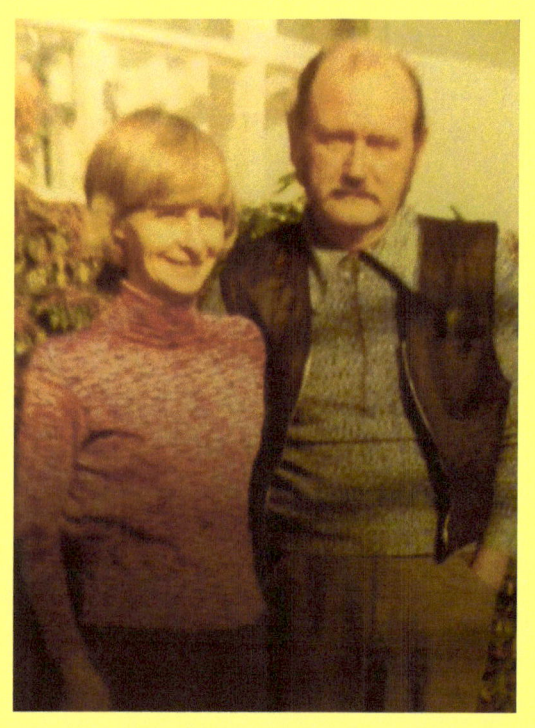

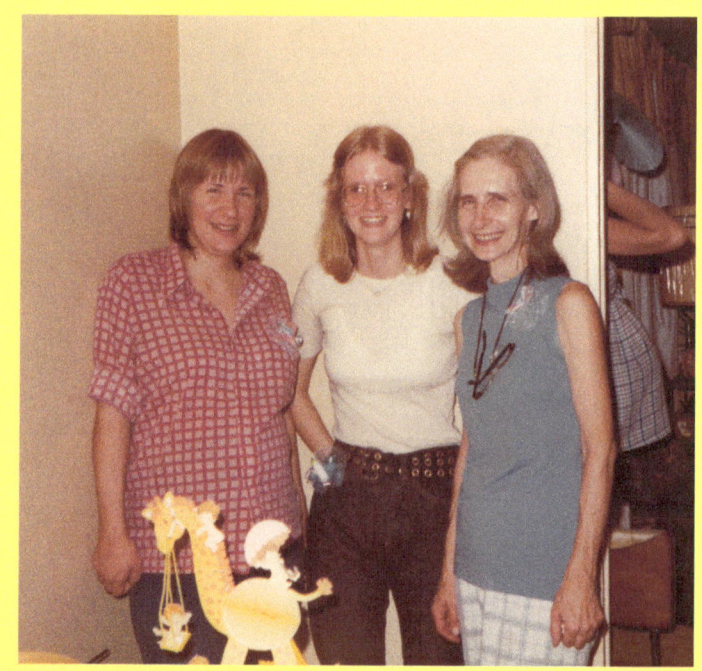

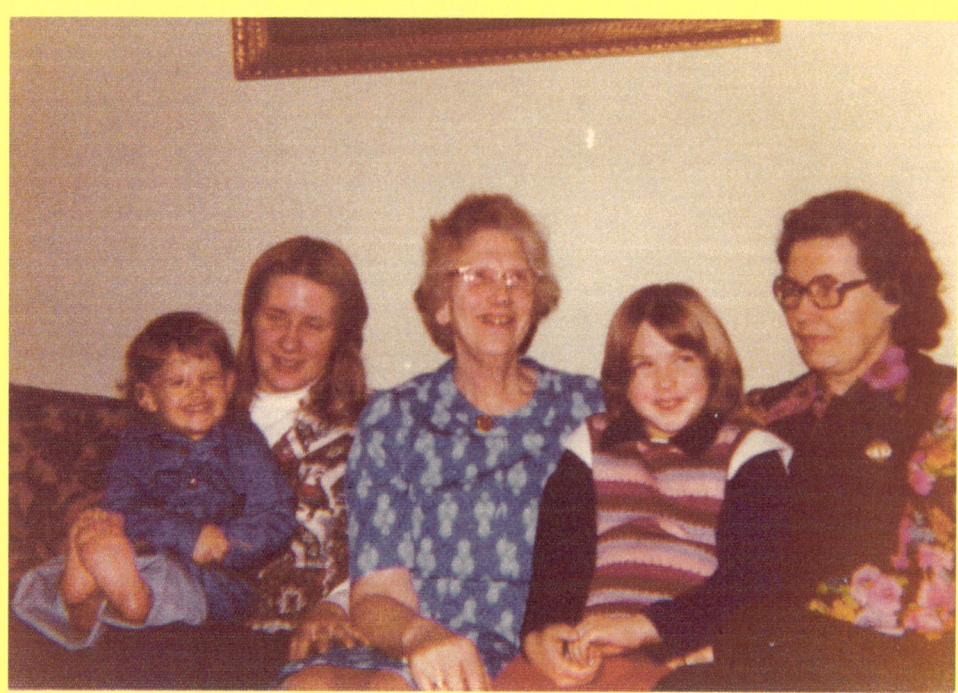

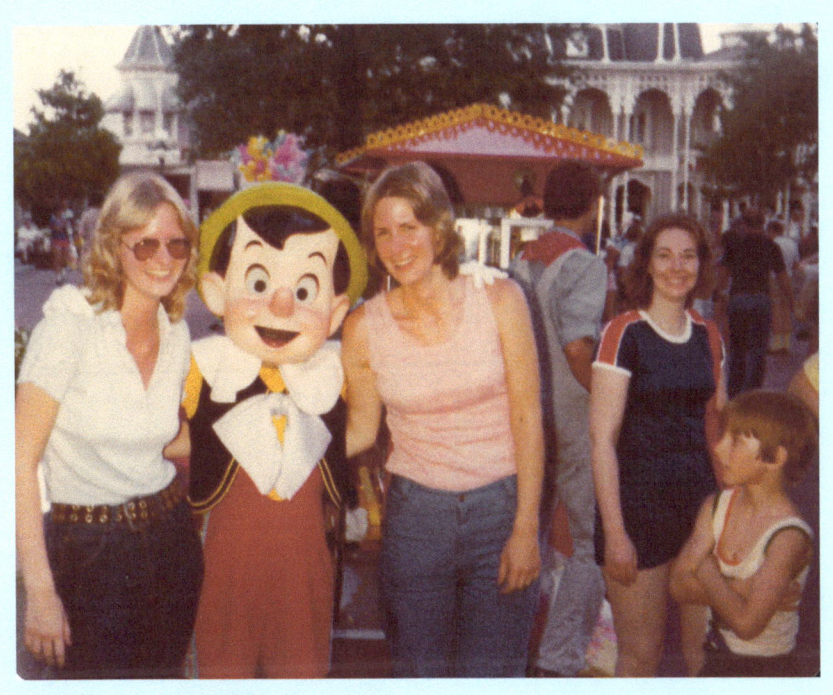

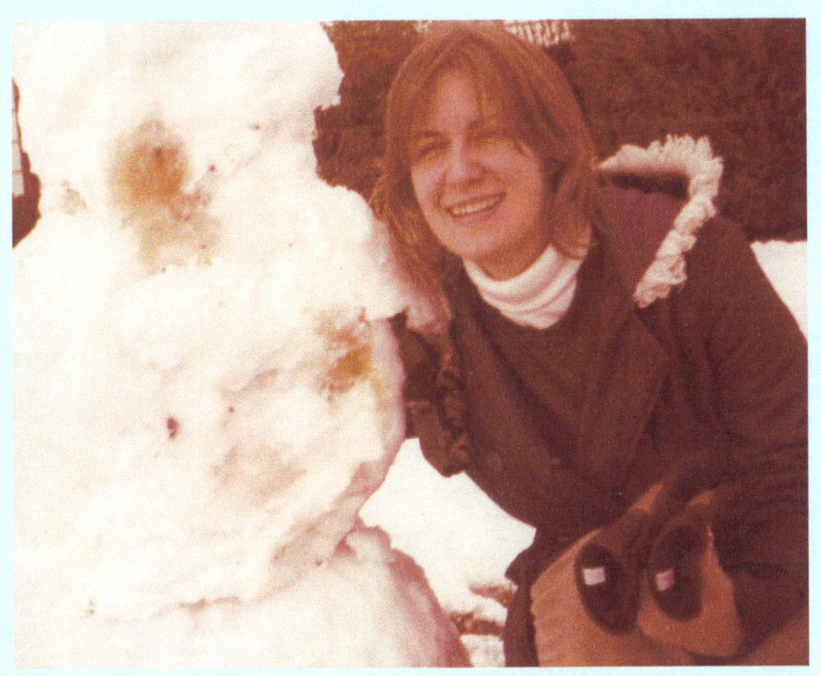

When everything goes to hell, the people who stand by you without flinching—they are your family.

– Jim Butcher

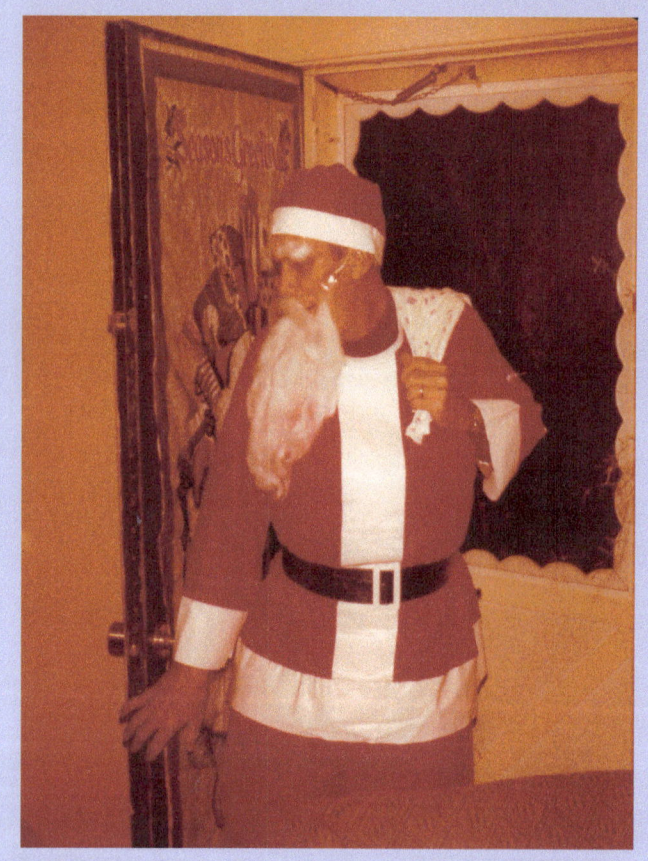

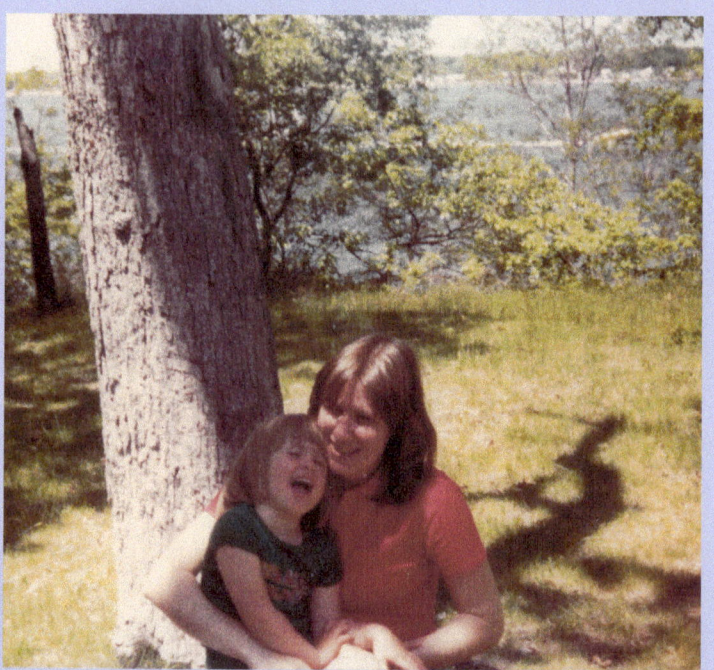

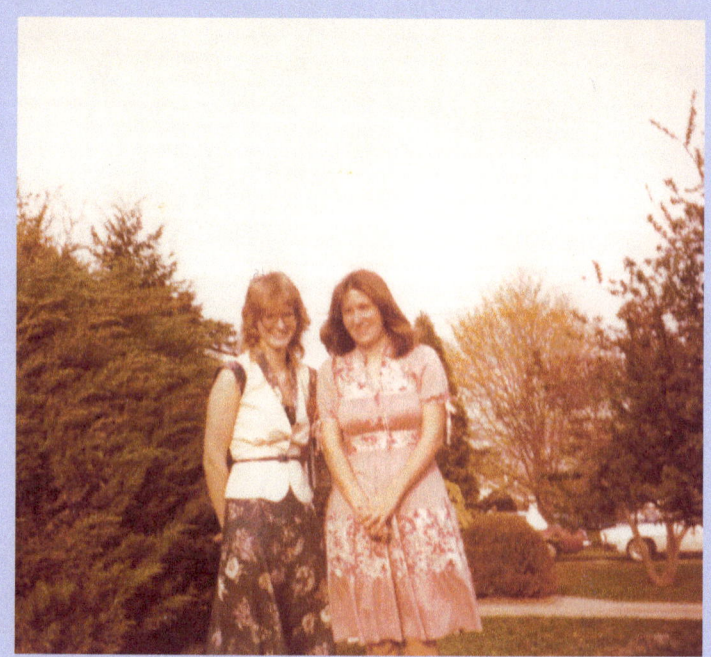

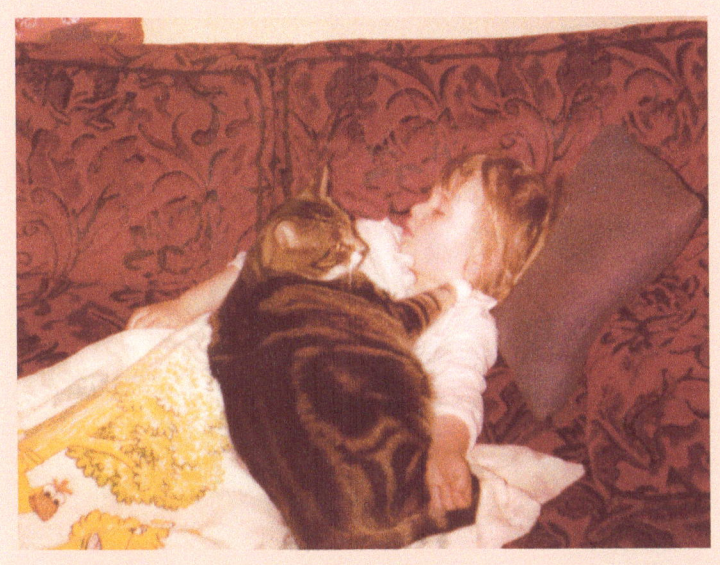

You don't choose your family. They are God's gift to you, as you are to them.

– Desmond Tutu

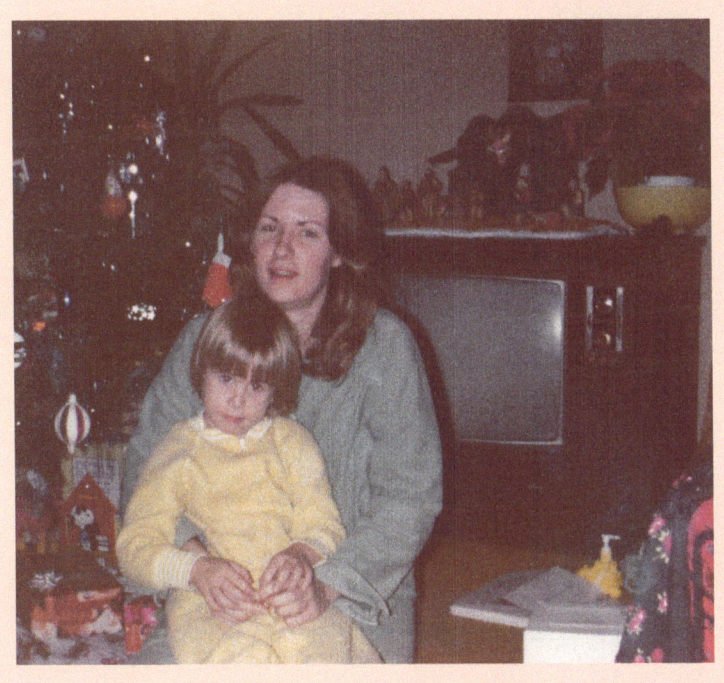

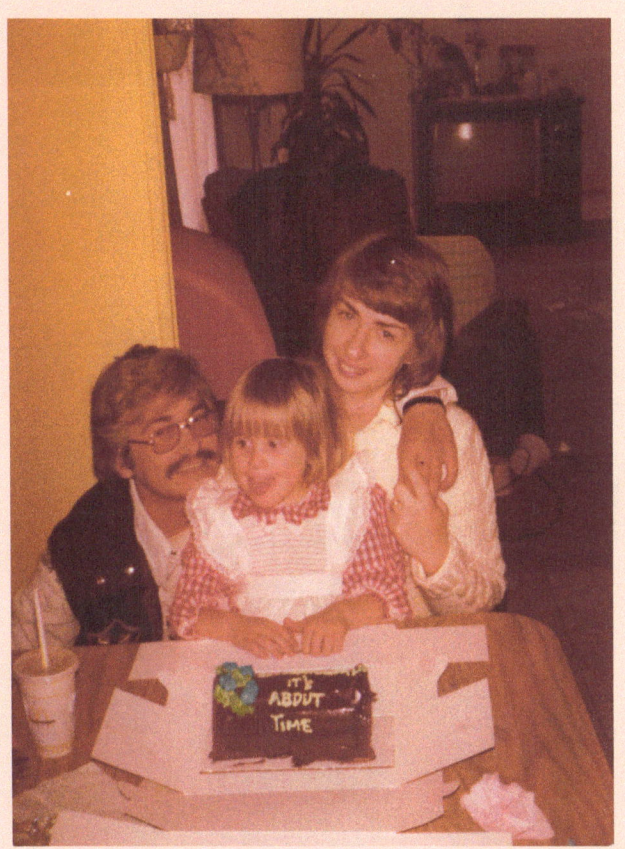

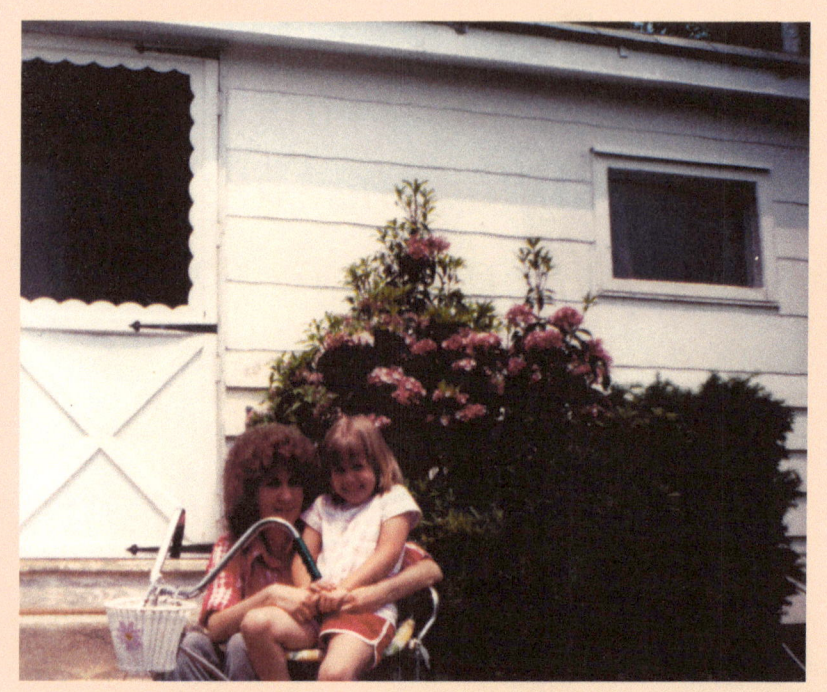

*Family is not an
important thing,
it's everything.*

– Michael J. Fox

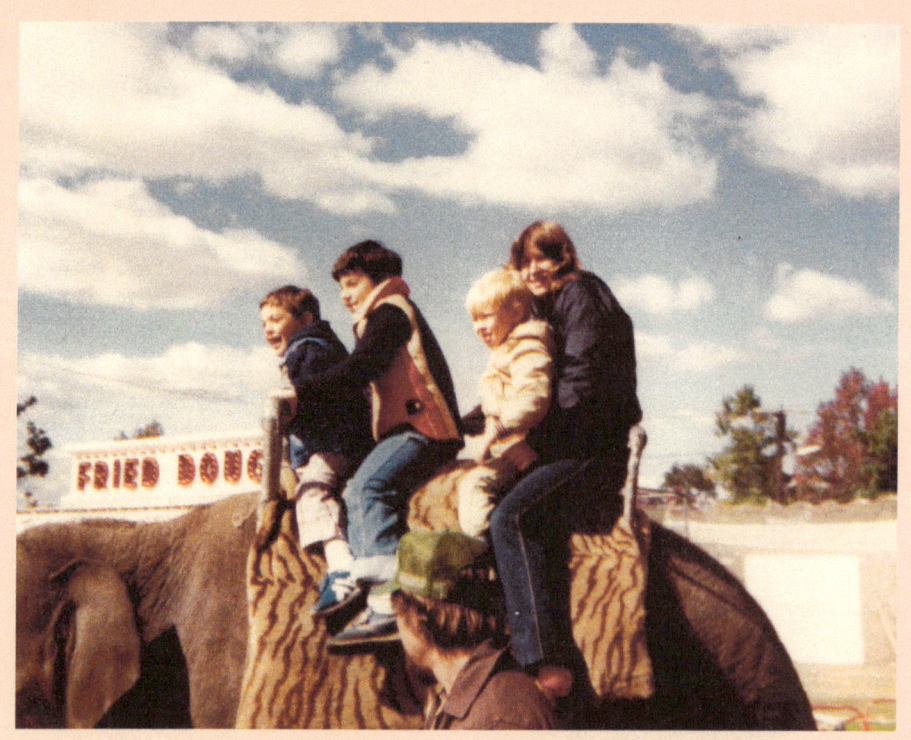

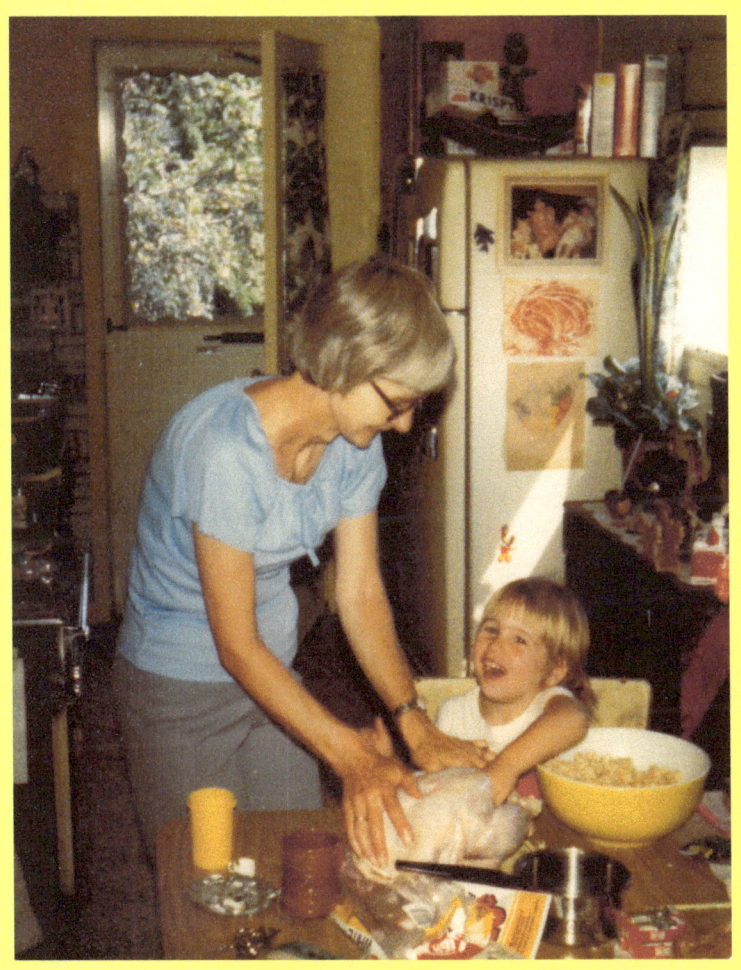

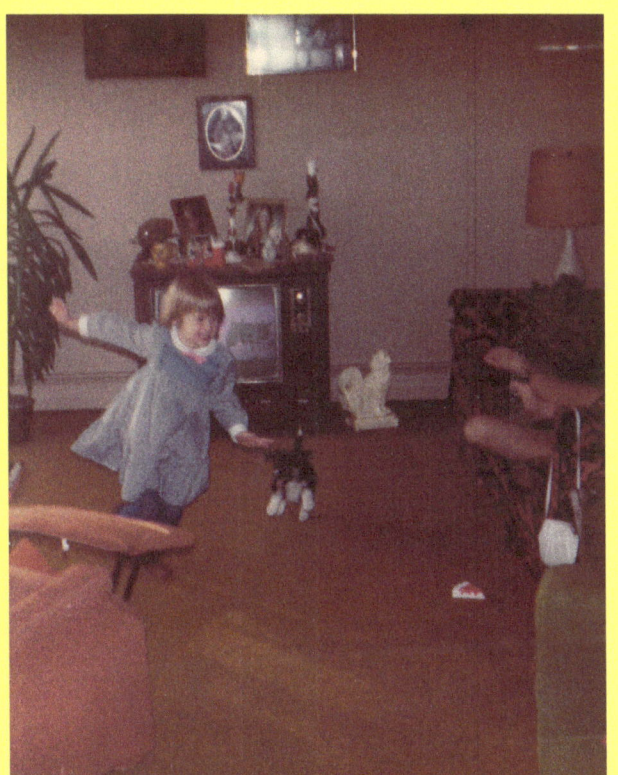

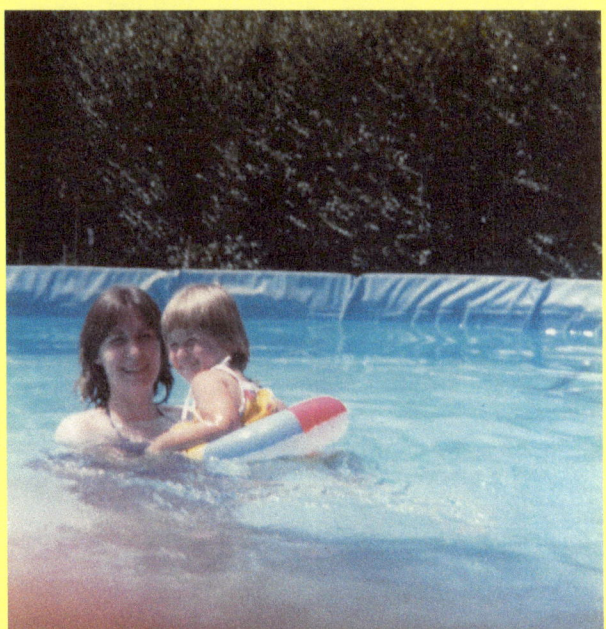

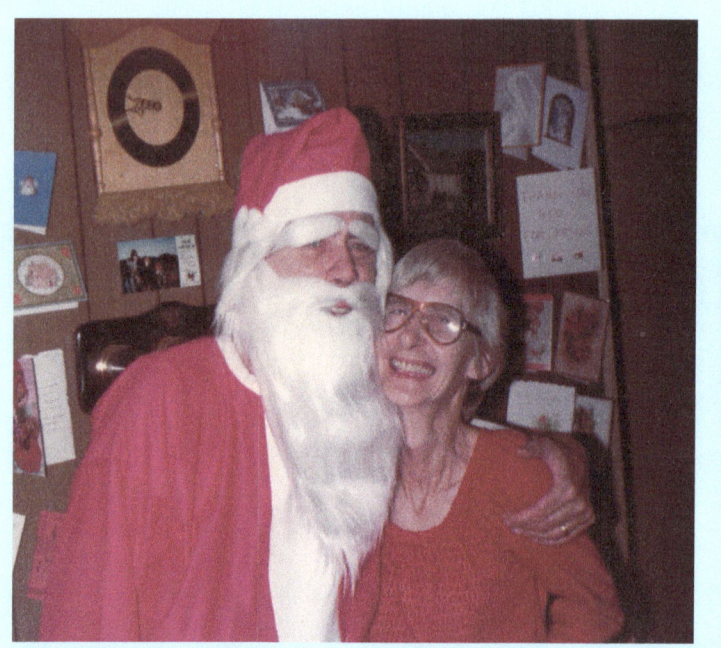

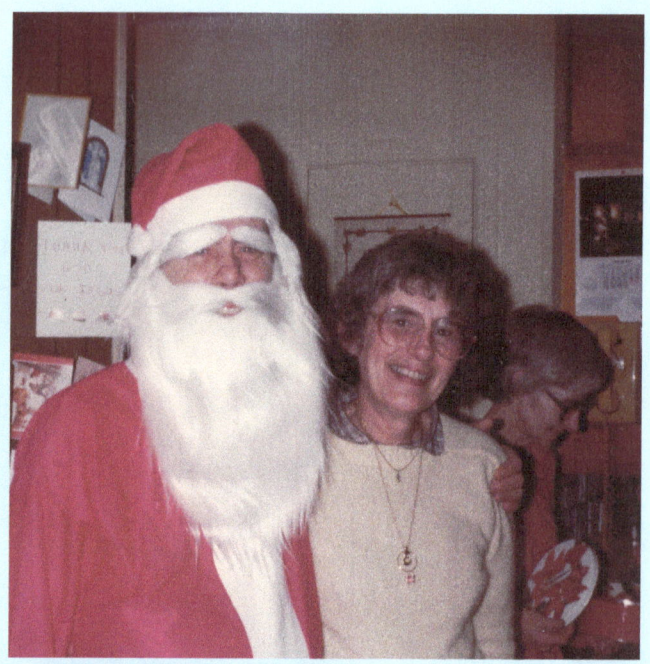

*I find the family the
most mysterious and
fascinating institution
of the world.*

– Amos Oz

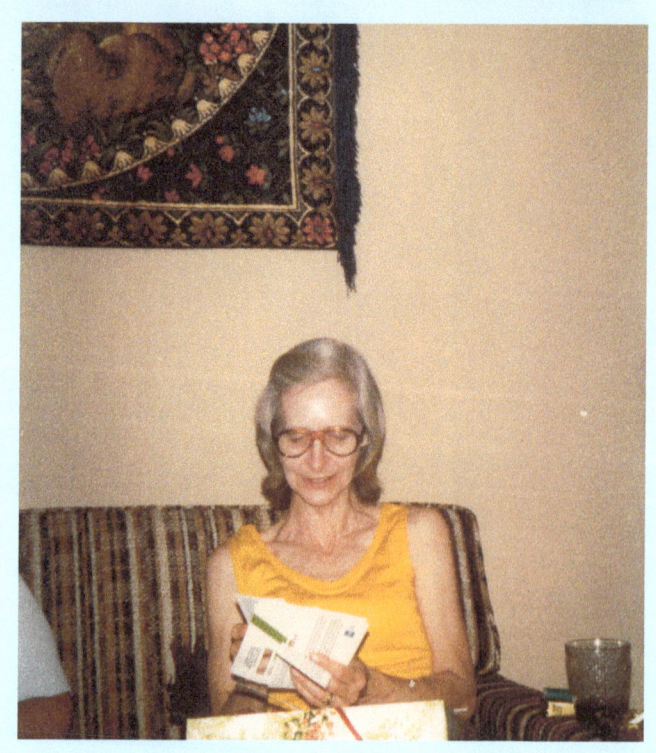

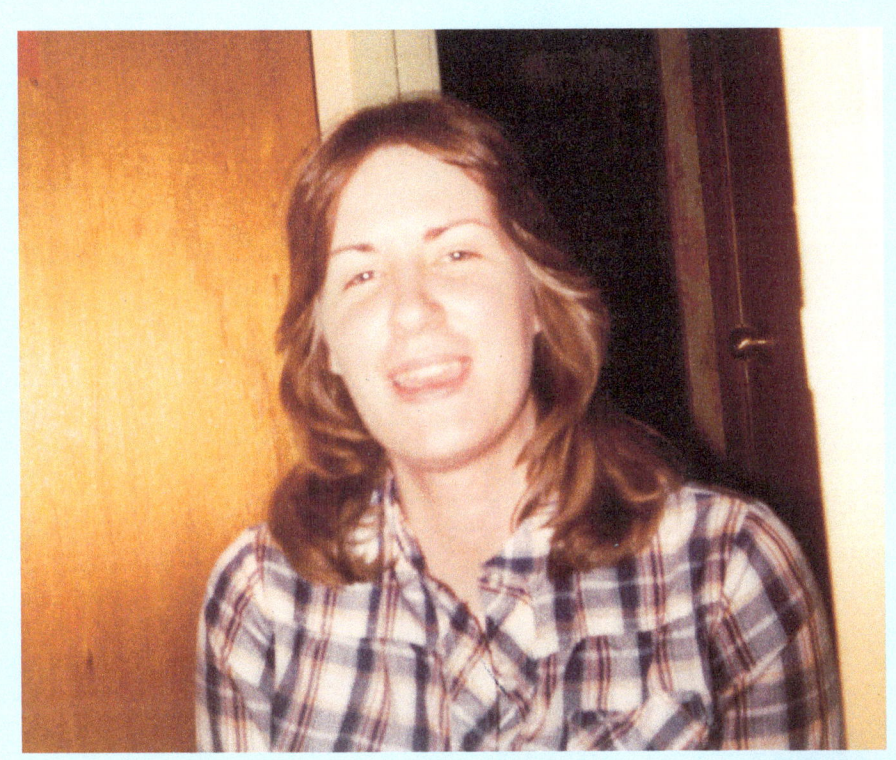

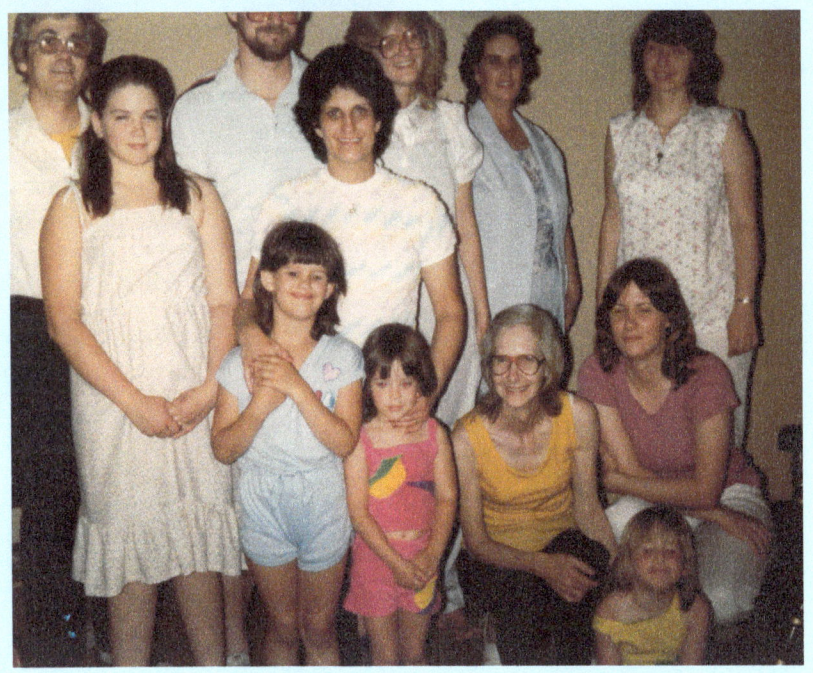

13

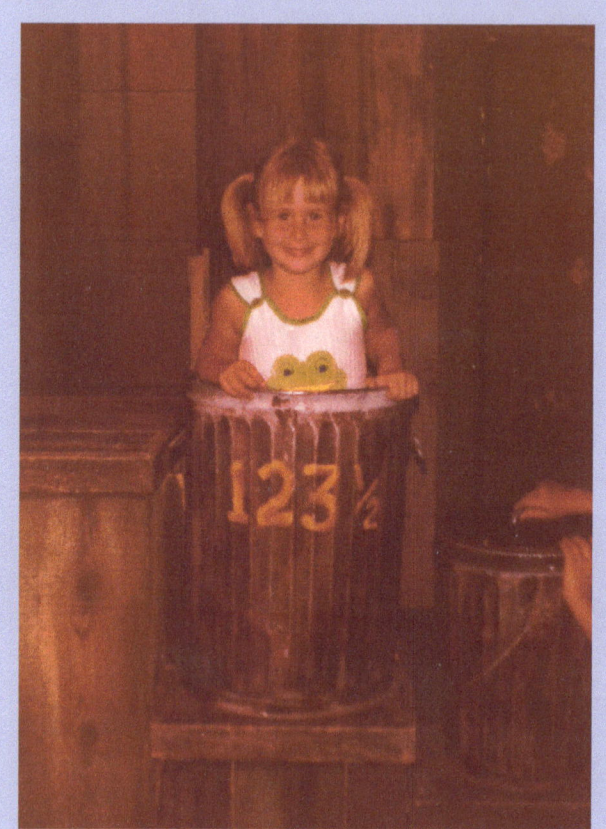

The strength of a family, like the strength of an army, is in its loyalty to each other.

– Mario Puzo

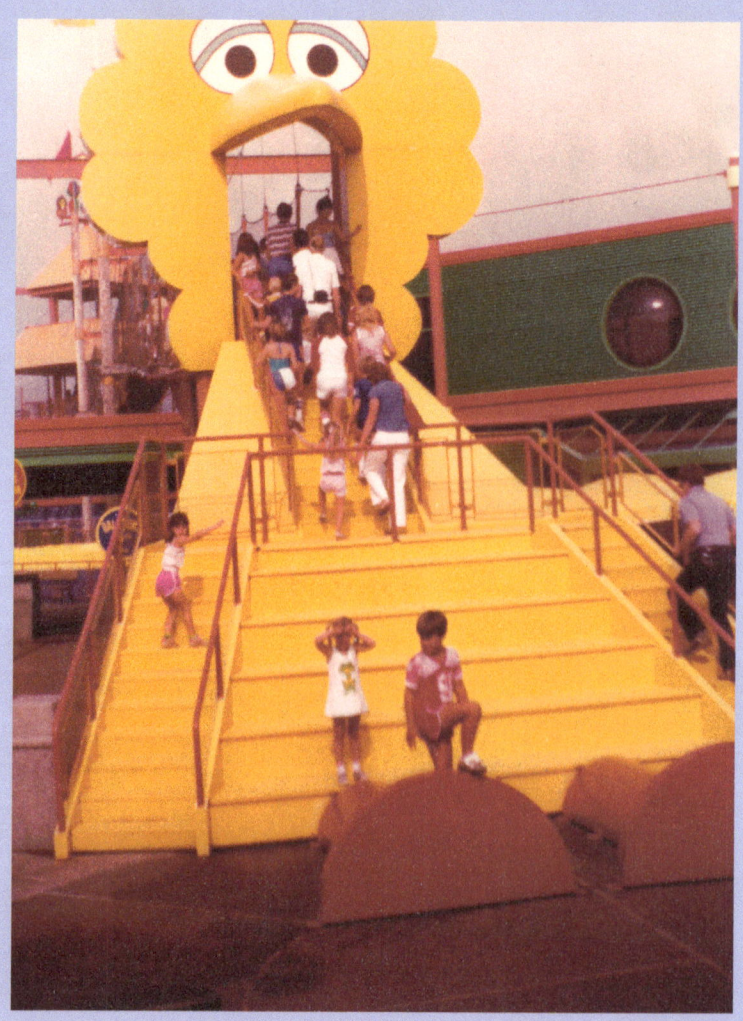

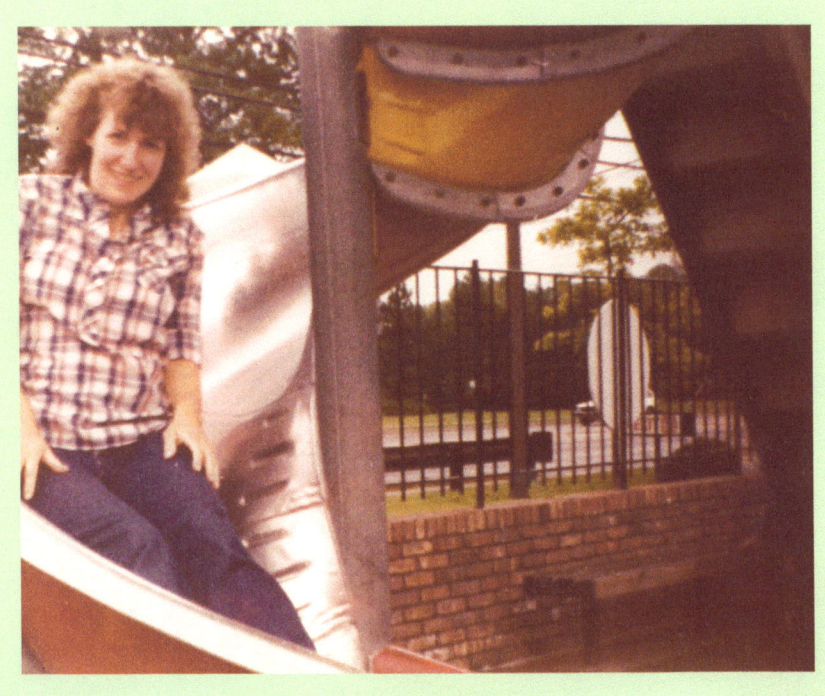

Cherish every moment with those you love at every stage of your journey.

– Jack Layton

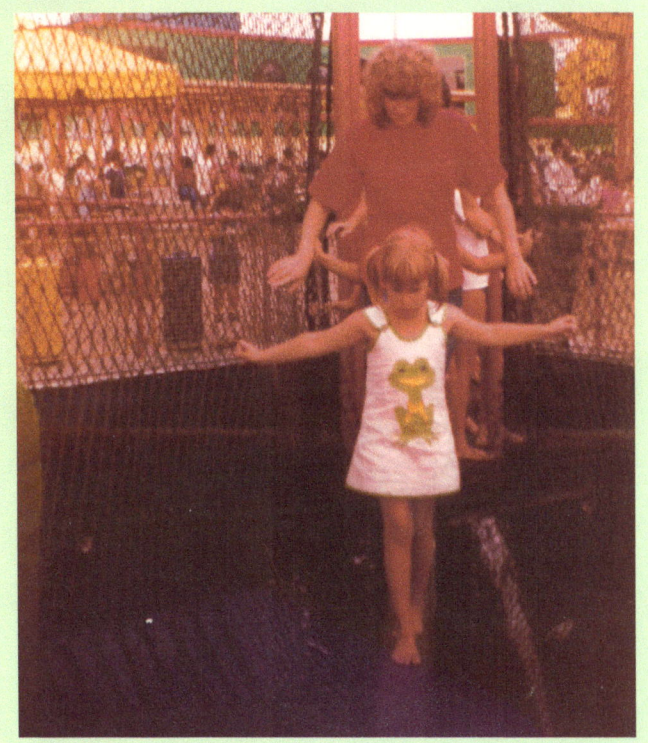

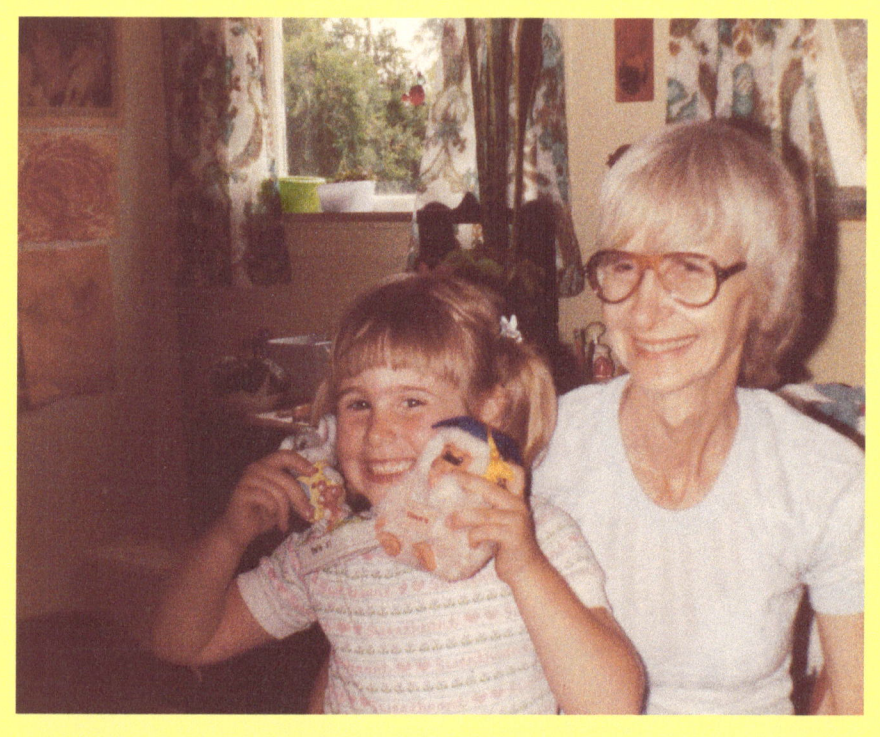

*Sticking with
your family is
what makes it a
family.*

– Mitch Albom

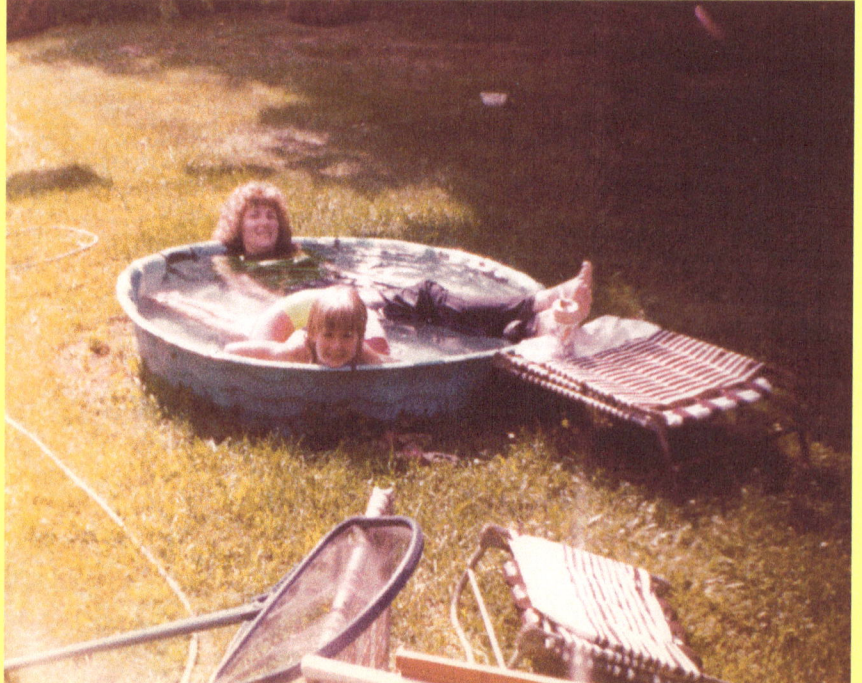

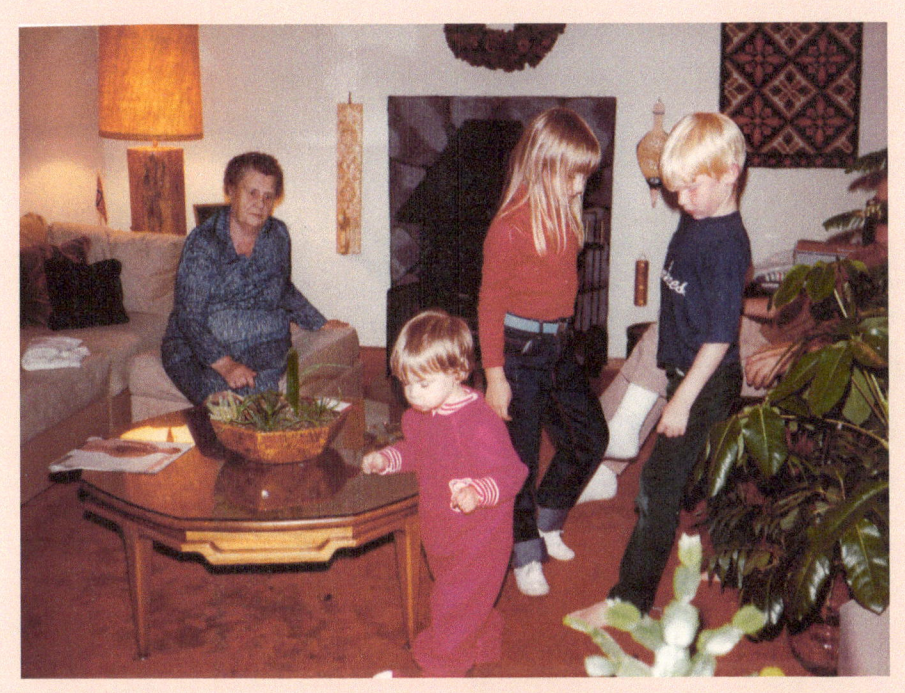

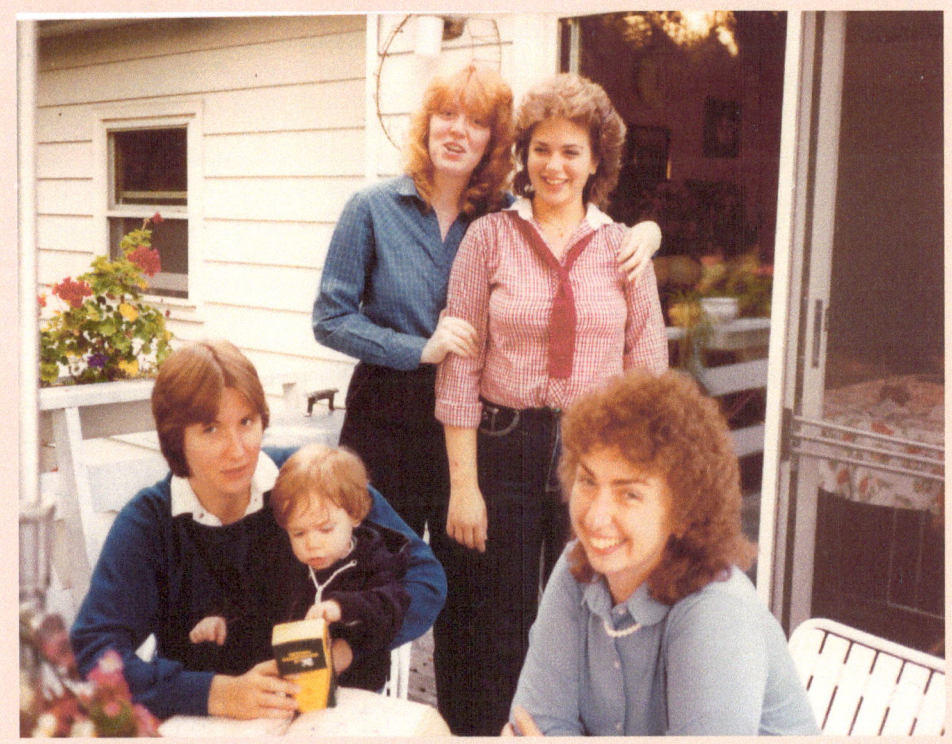

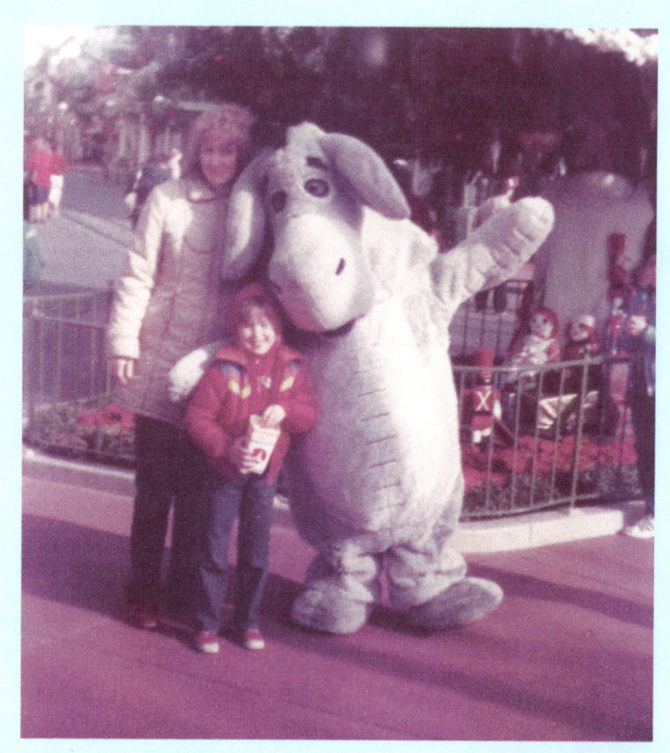

Family where life begins & love never ends.

– Unkown

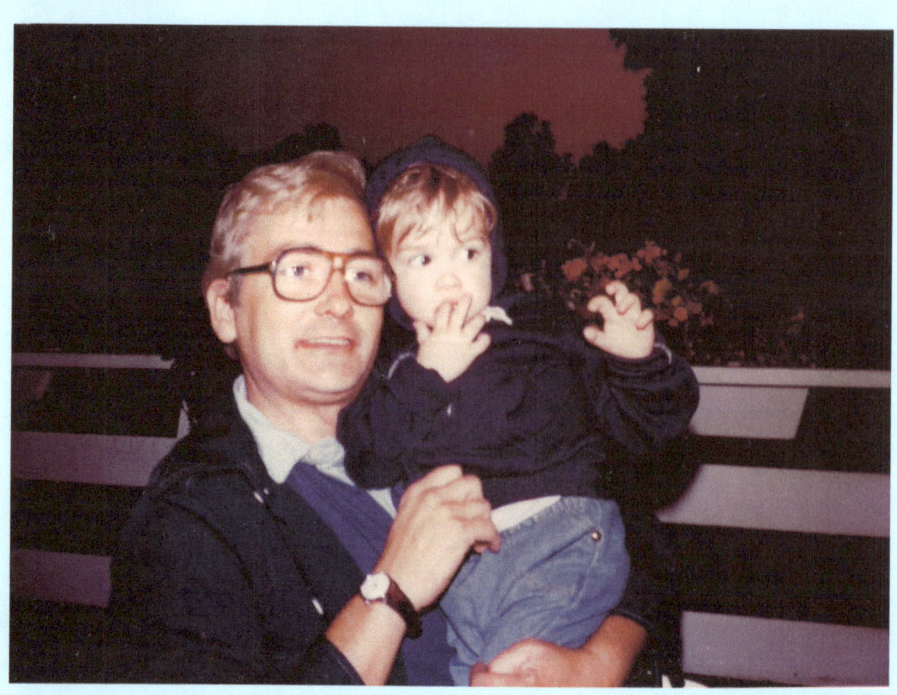

In family life, love is the oil that eases friction, the cement that binds closer together, and the music that brings harmony.

– Friedrich Nietzche

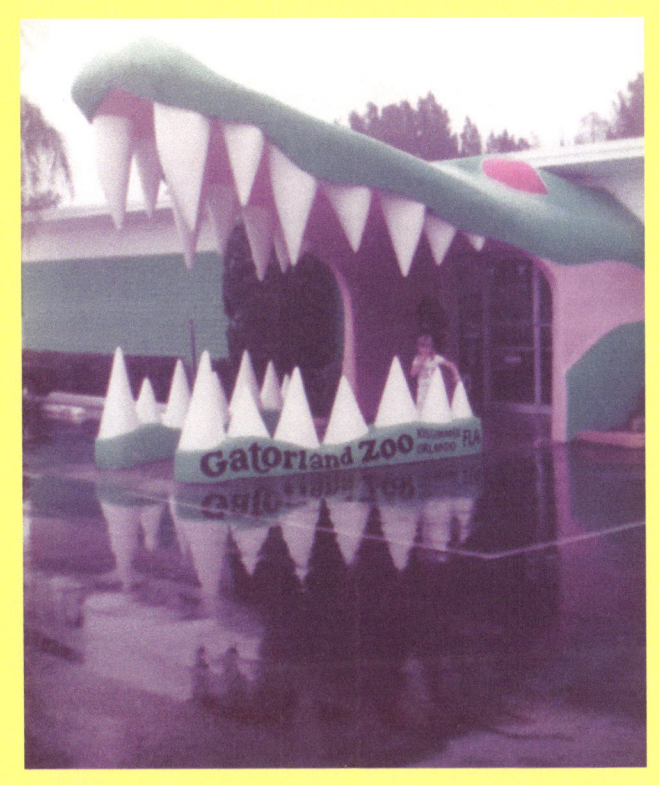

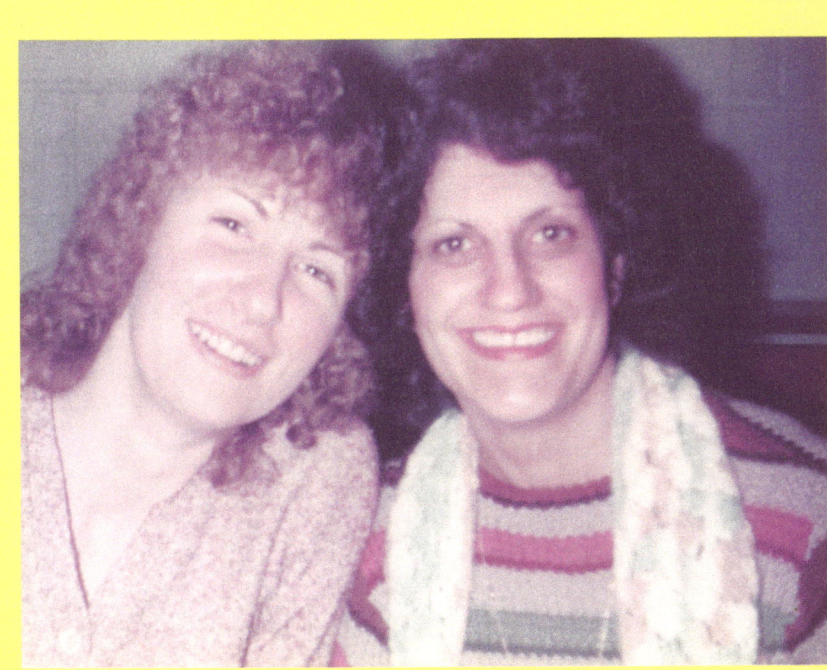

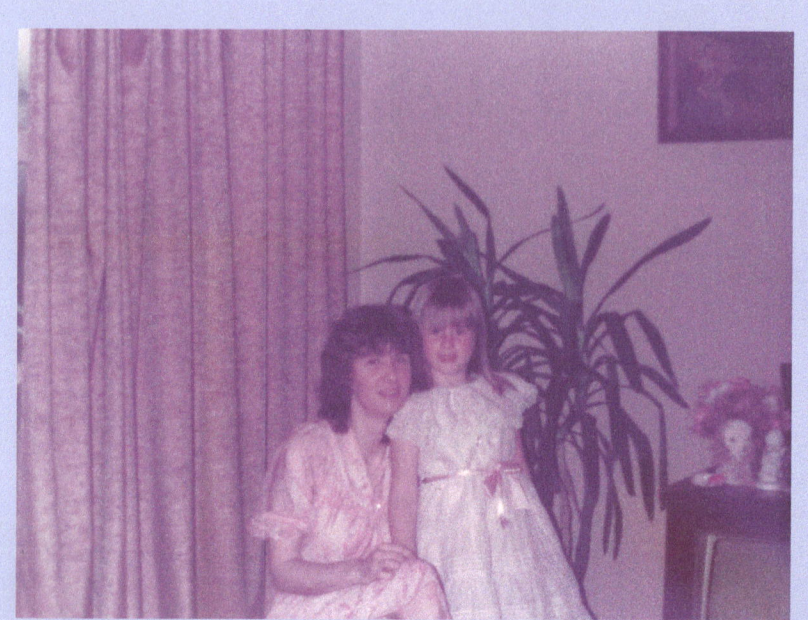

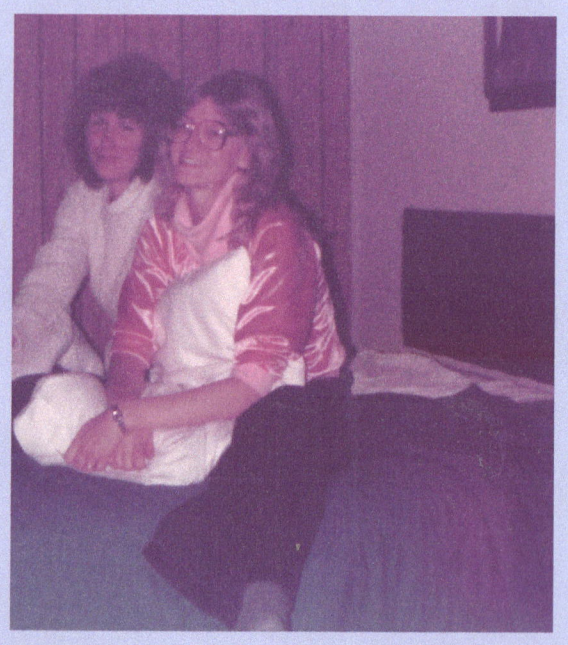

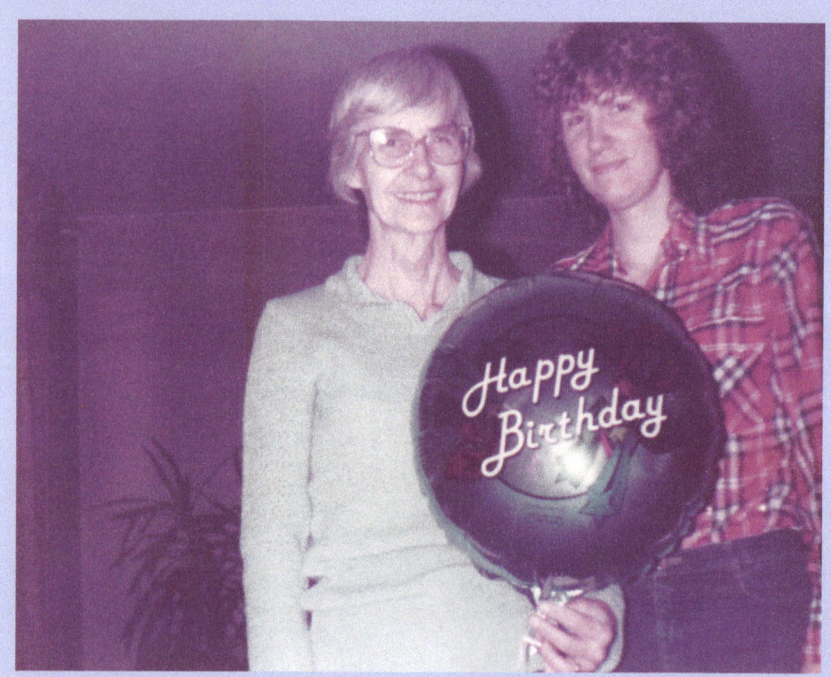

*The love of family
and the admiration
of friends is much
more important
than wealth and
privilege.*

– Charles Kuralt

20

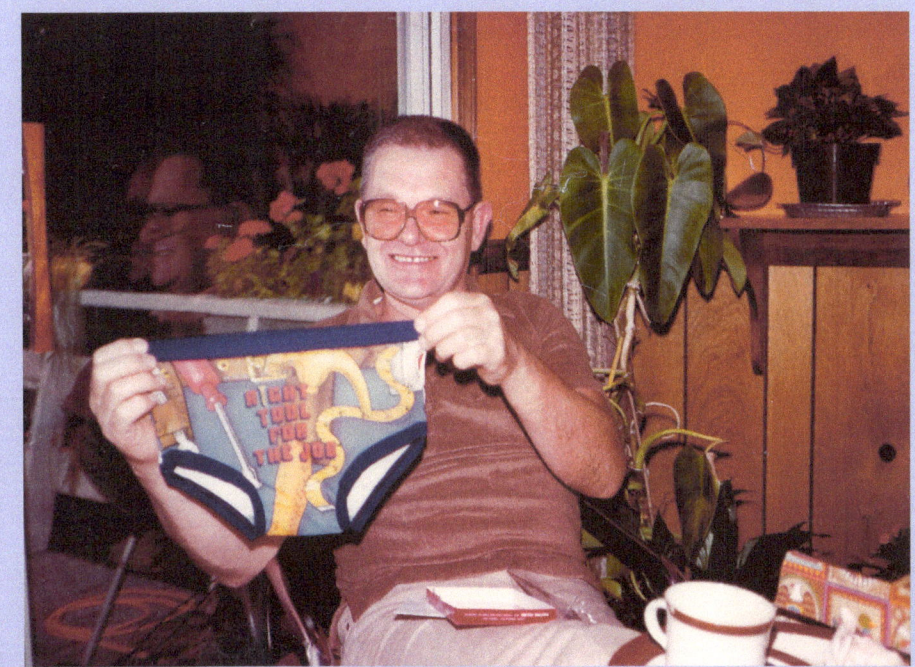

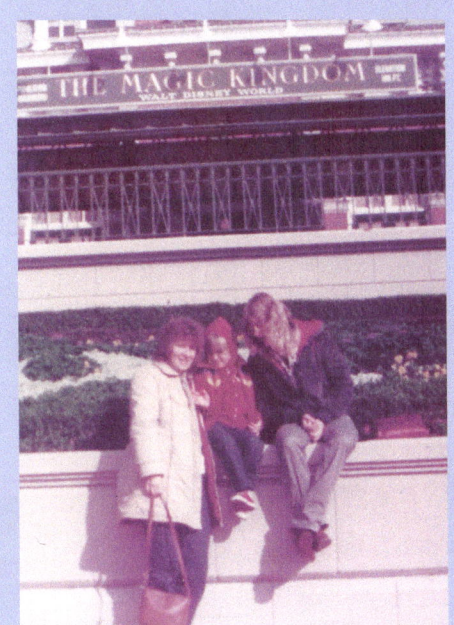

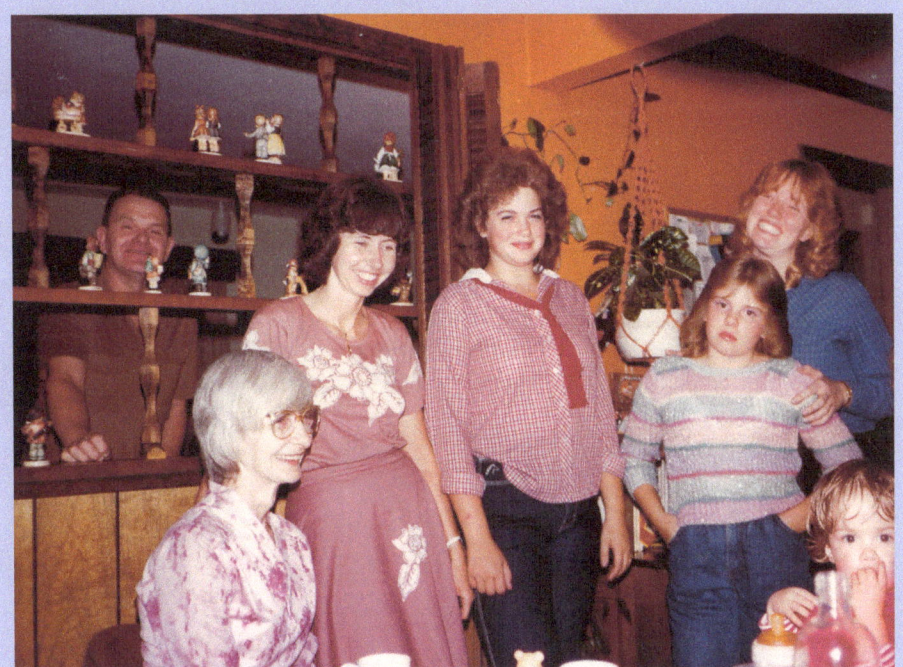

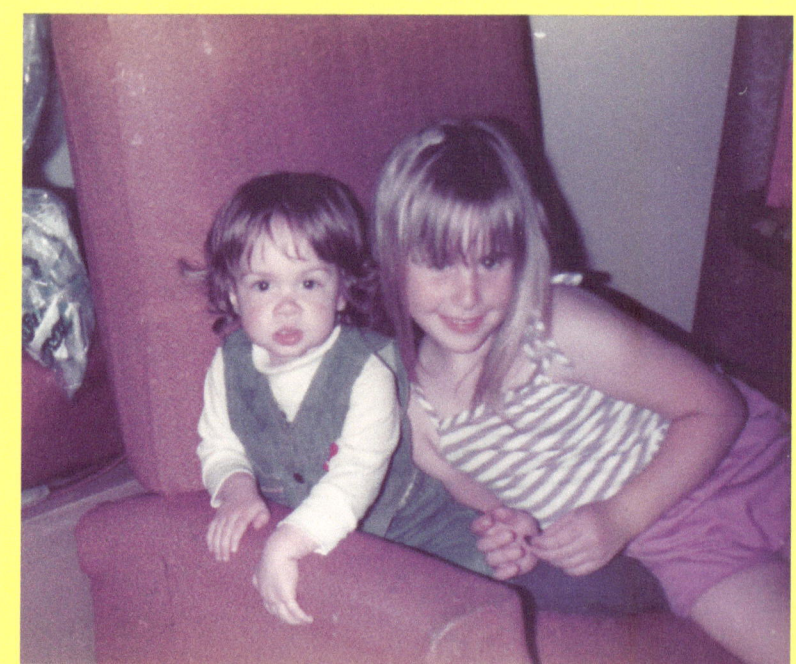

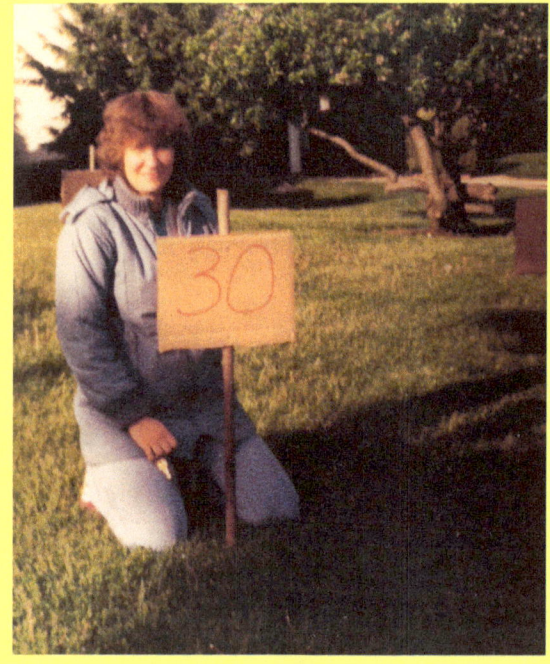

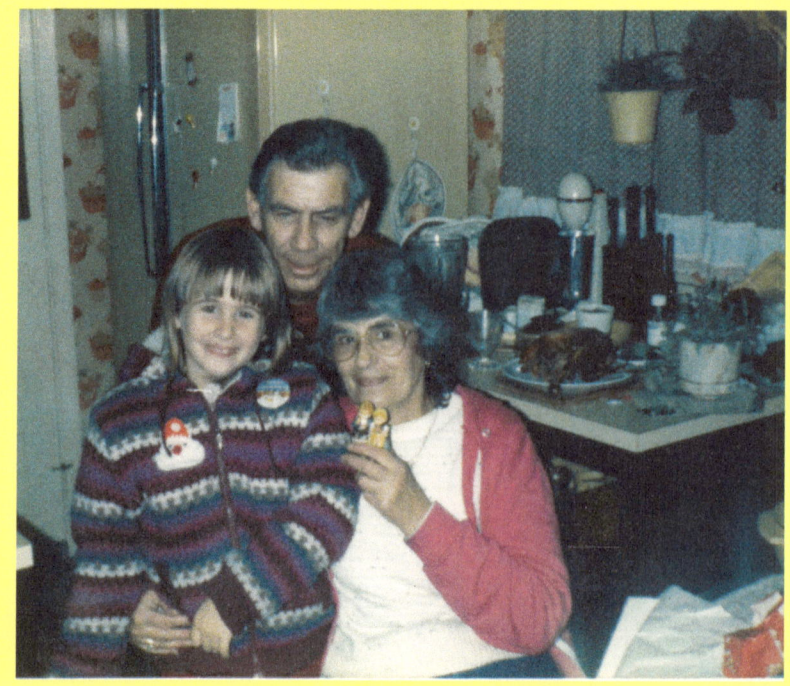

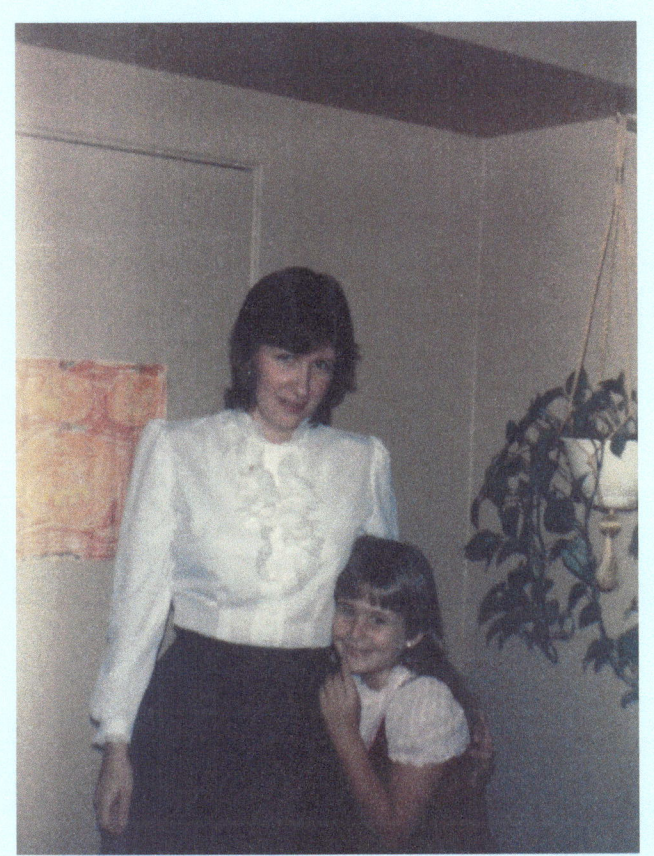

Parents were the only ones obligated to love you; from the rest of the world you had to earn it.

– Ann Brashares

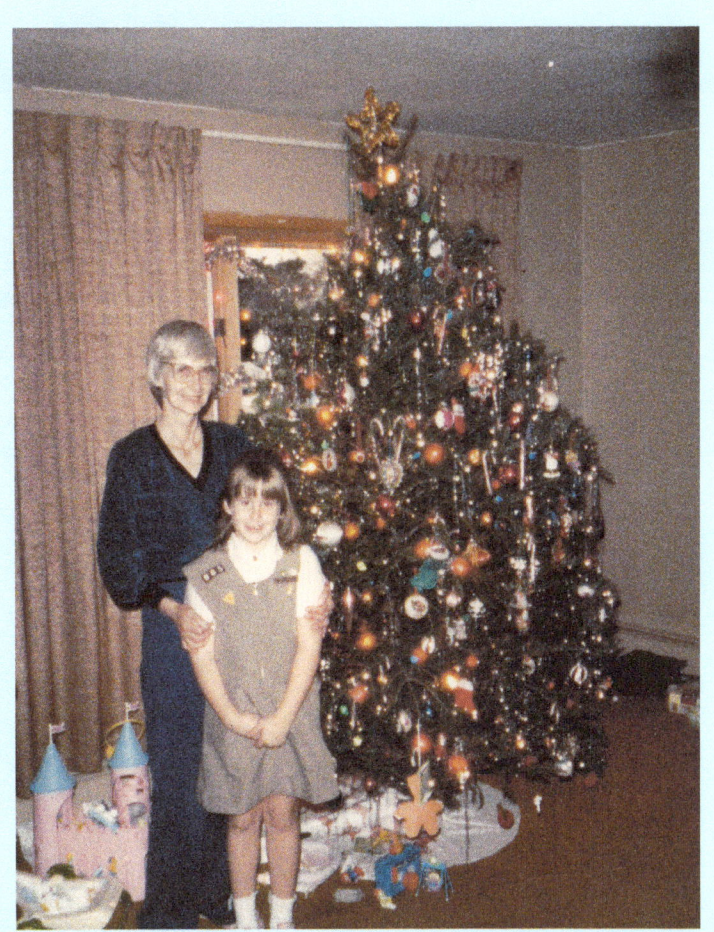

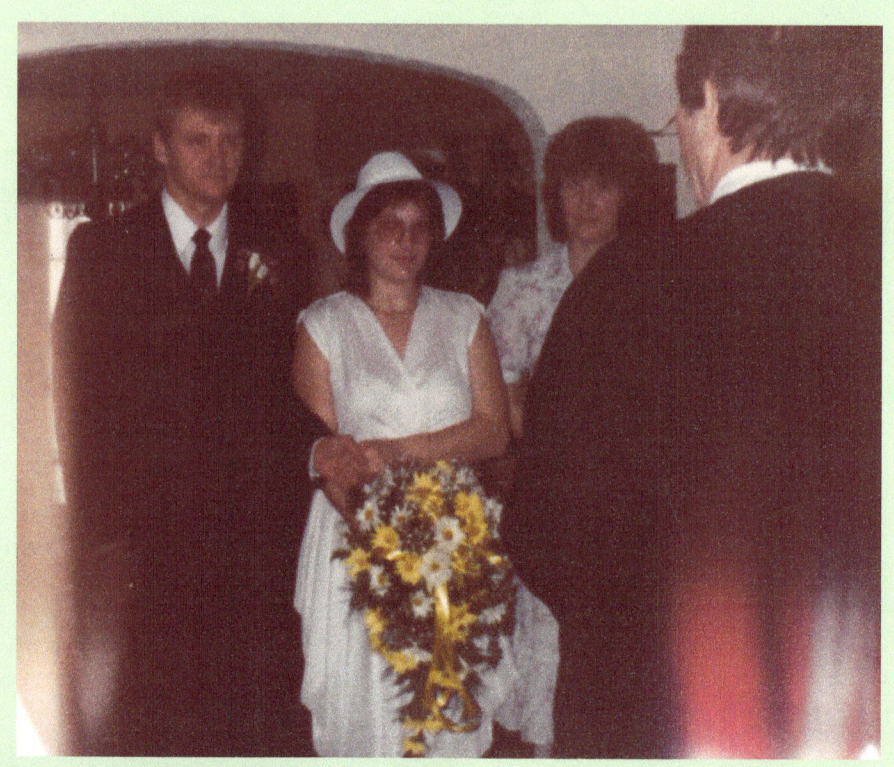

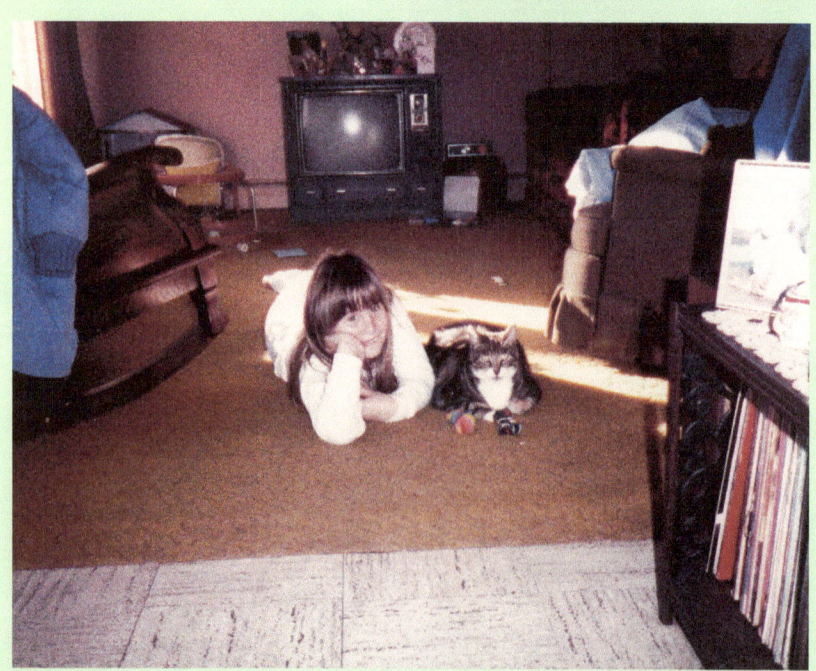

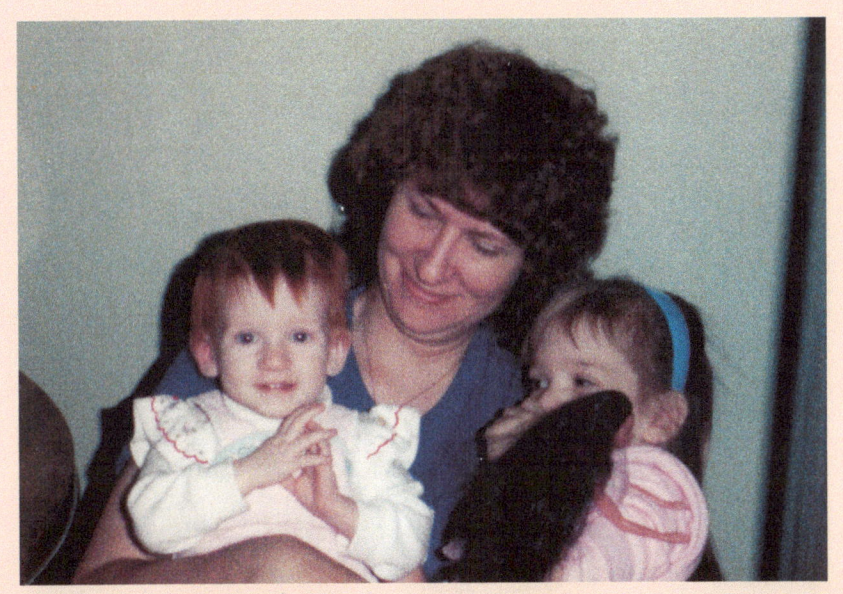

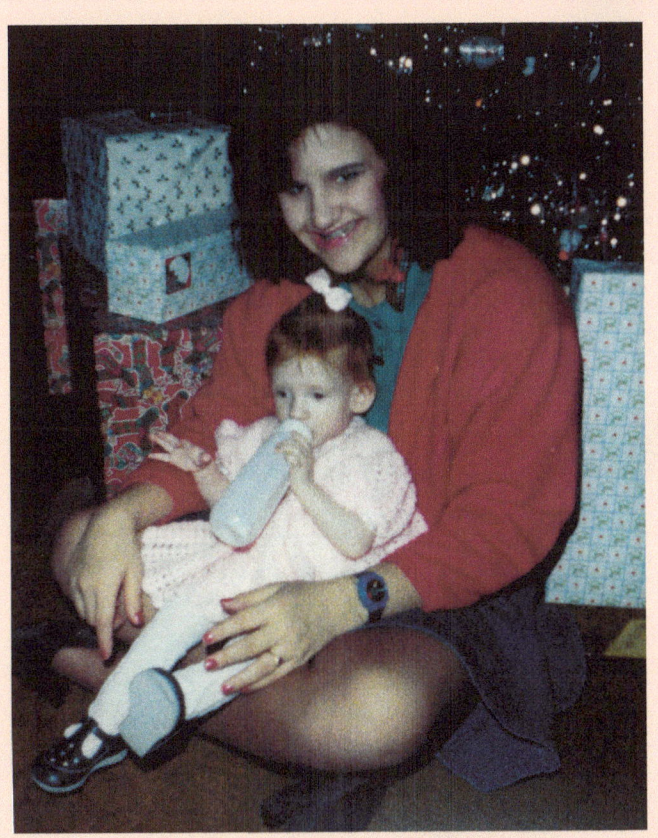

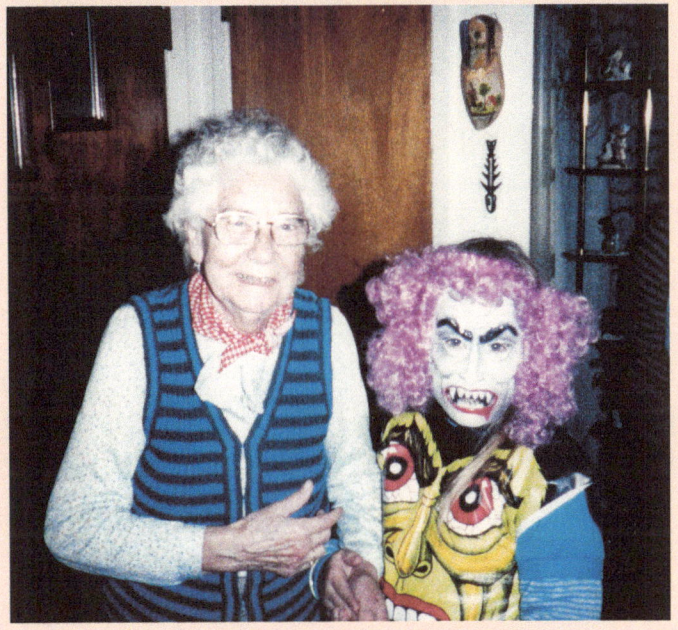

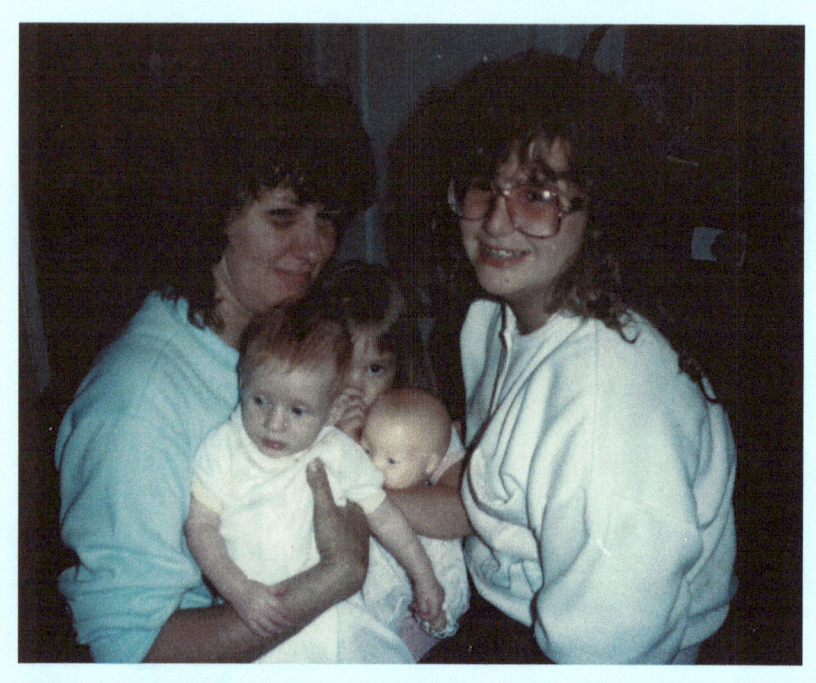

The love of a family is
life's greatest blessings.

– Unkown

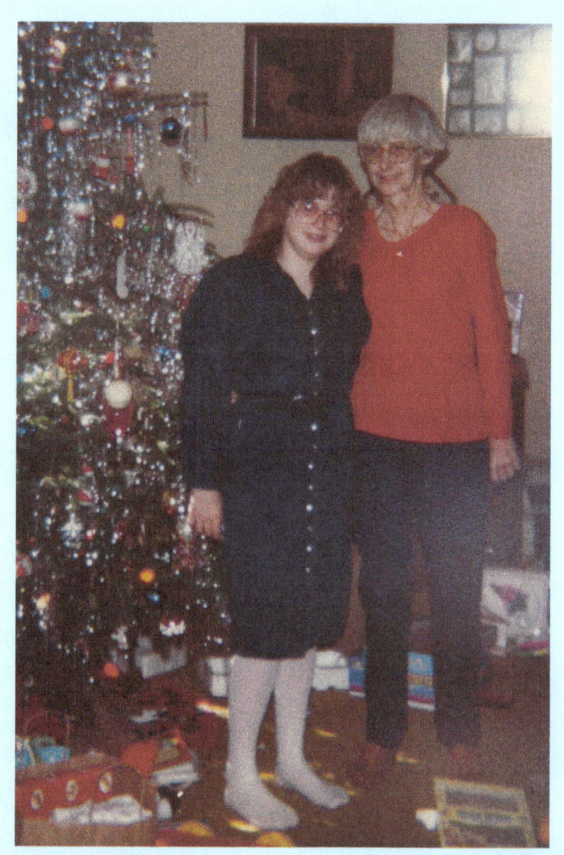

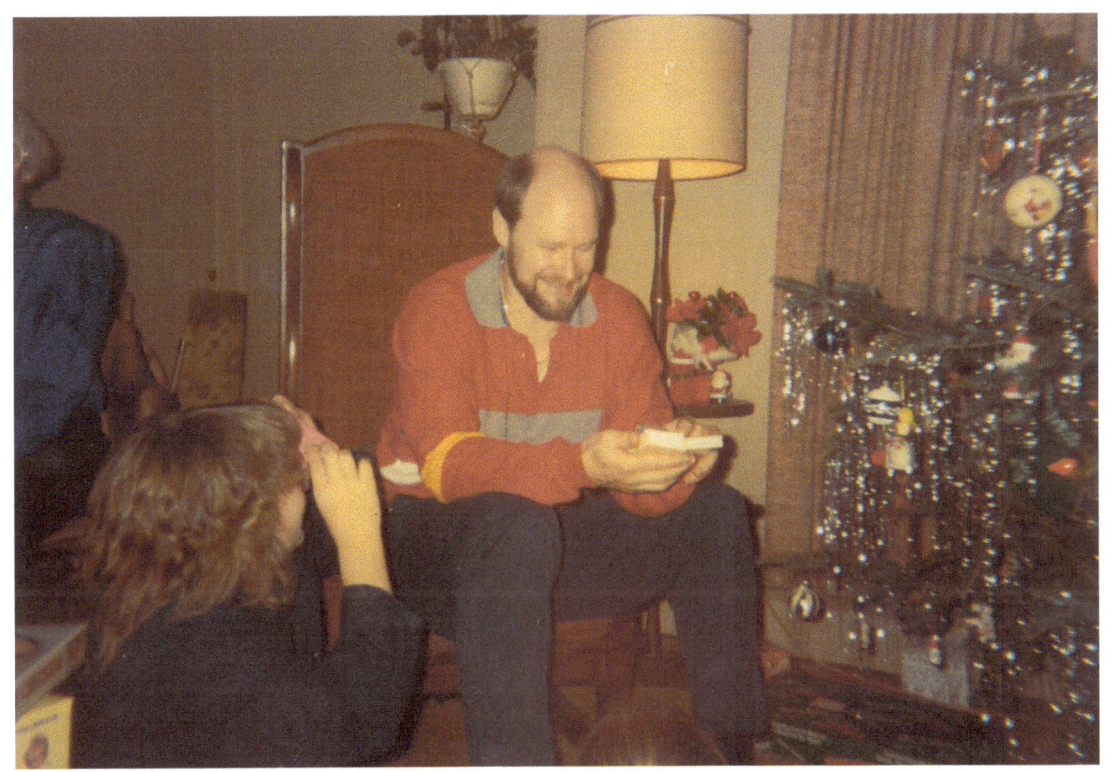

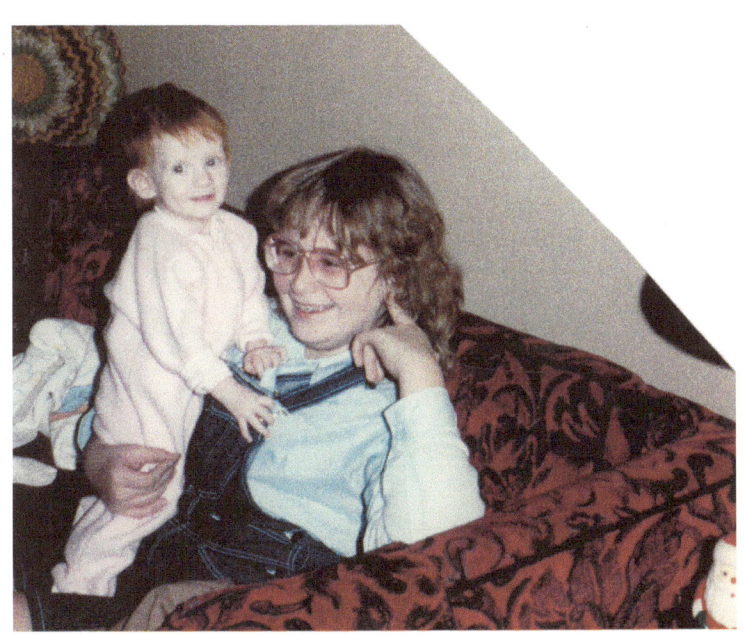

Love makes a family.

– Gigi Kaeser

27

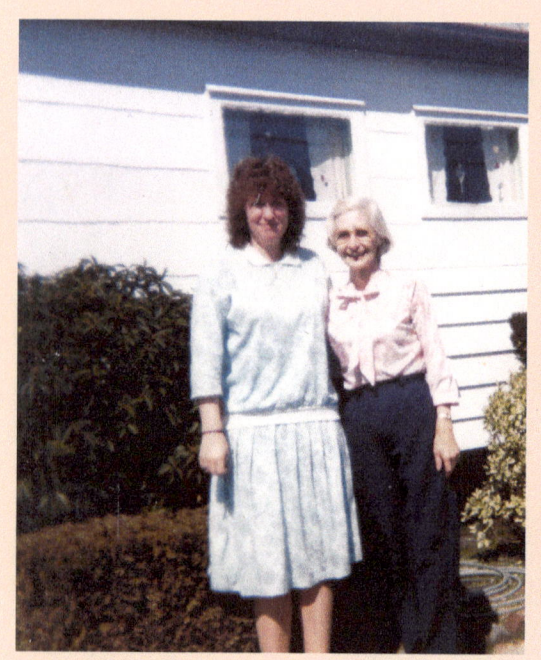
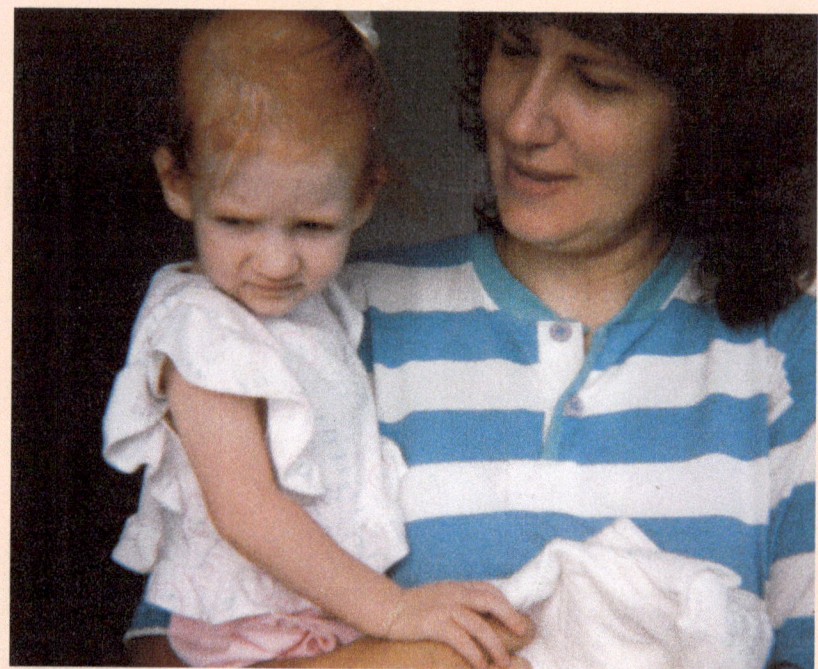
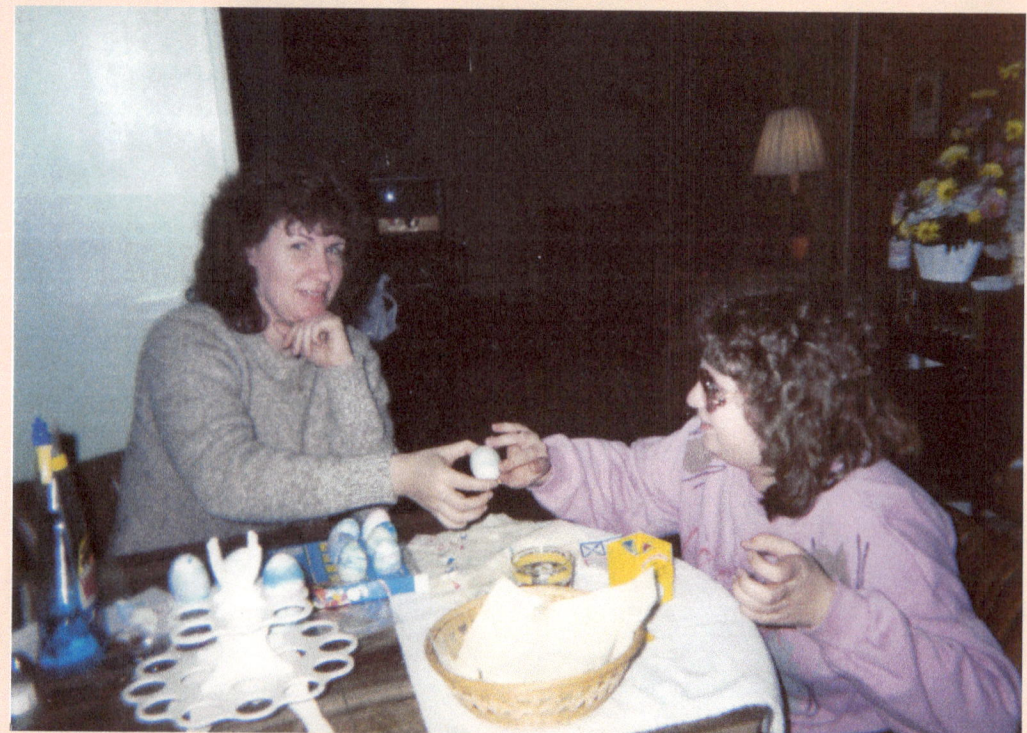

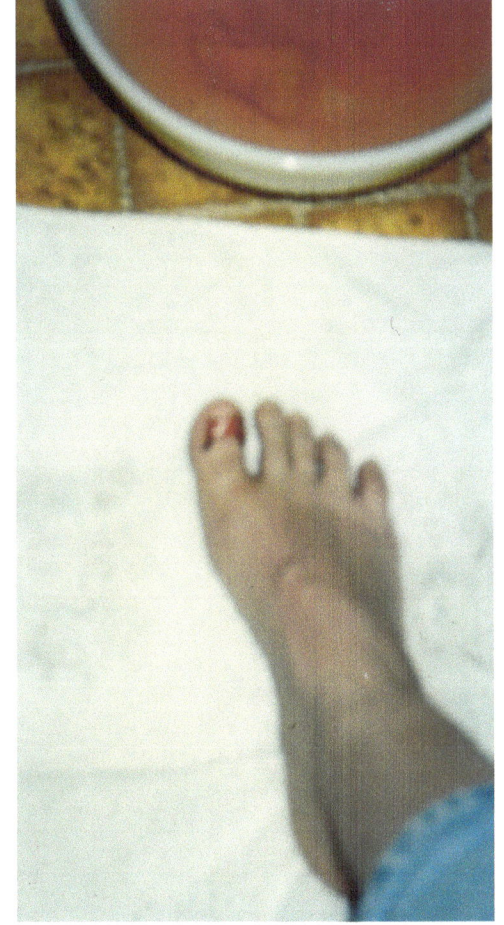

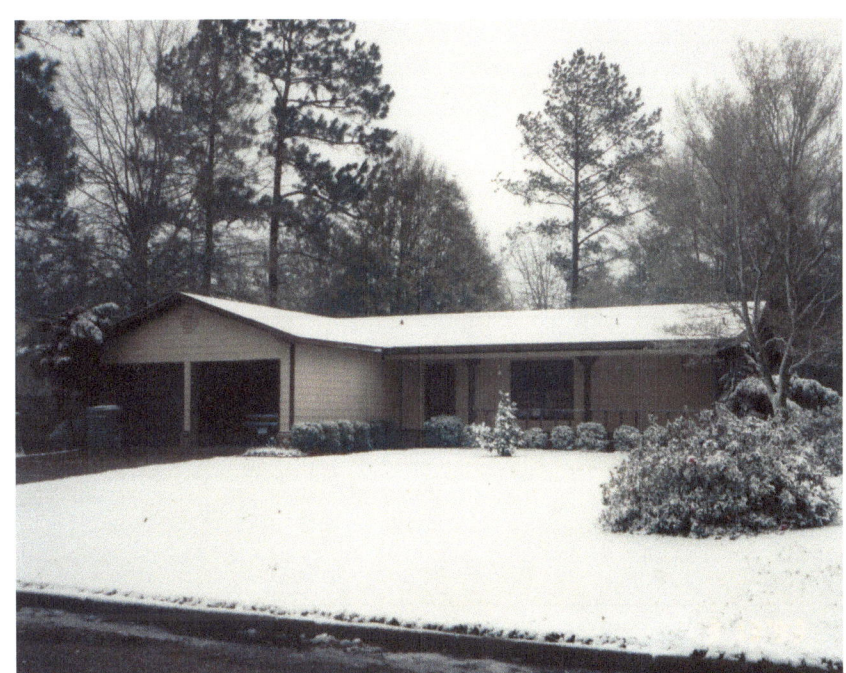

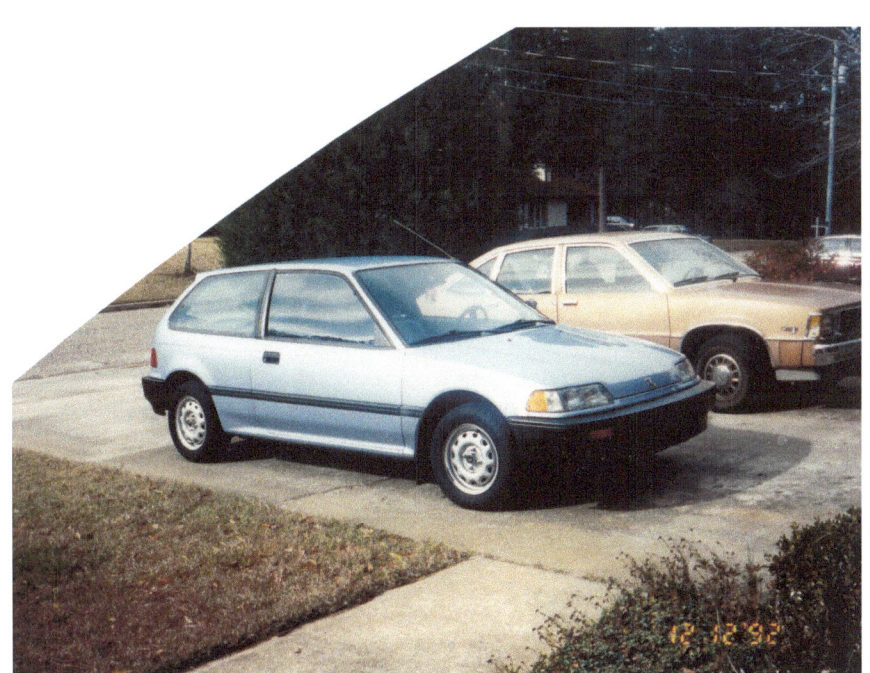

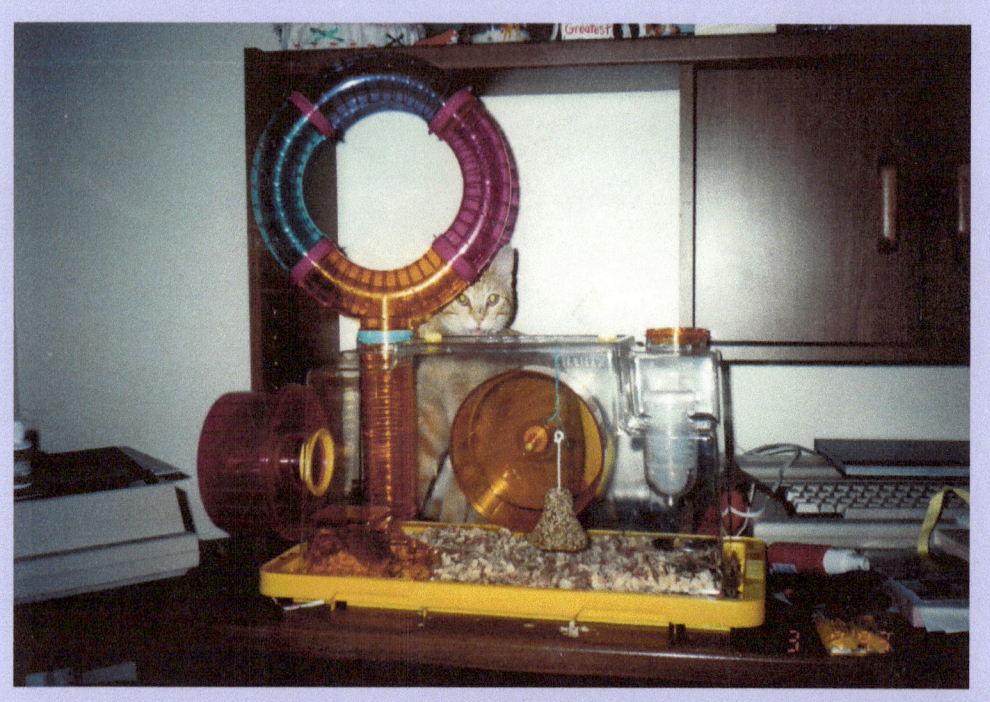

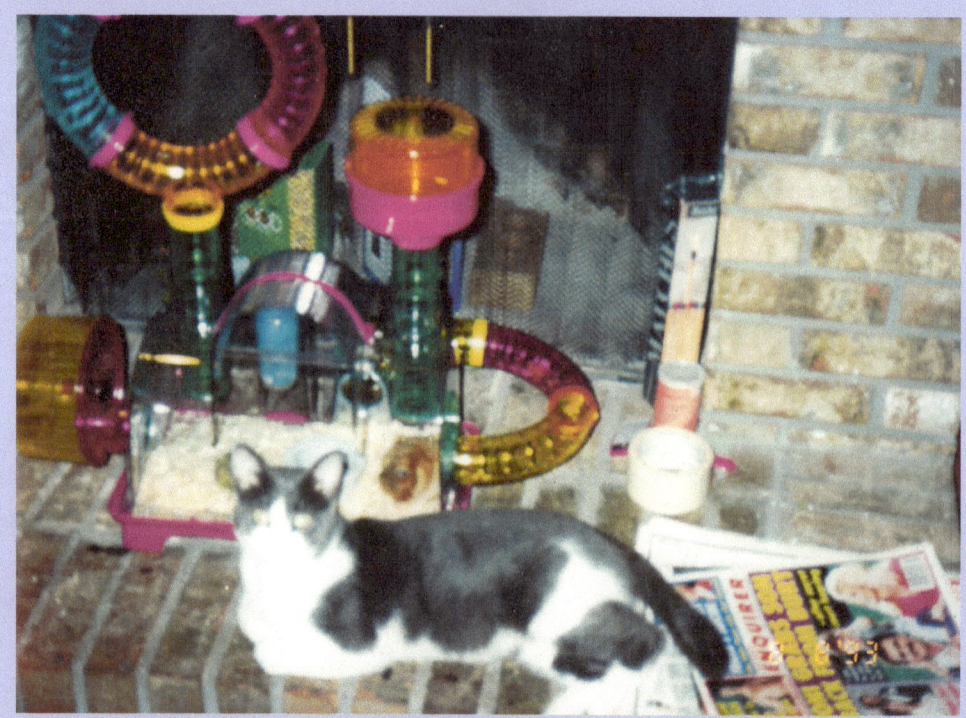

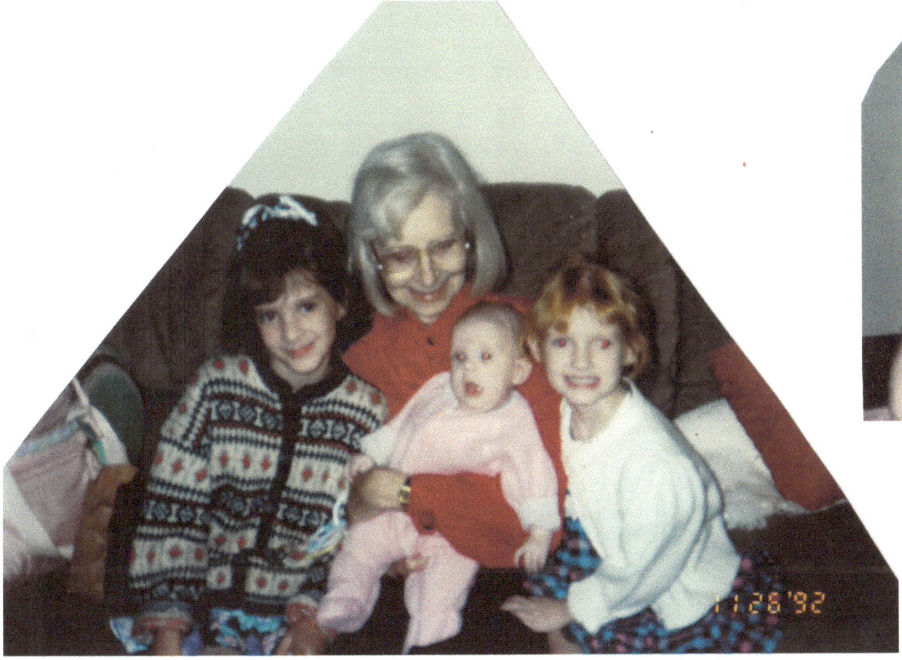

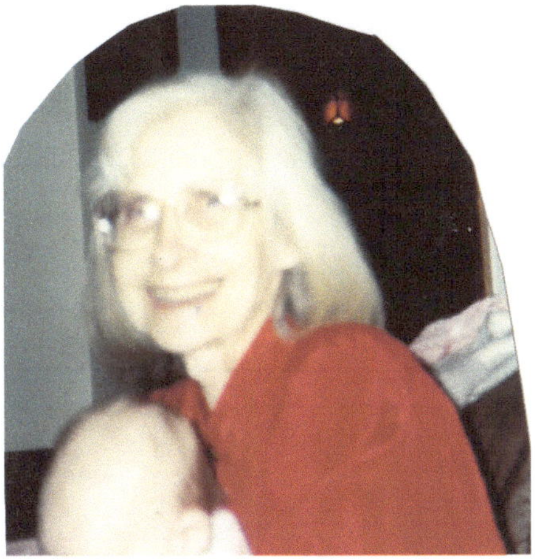

Family is what grounds you.

– Angelina Jolie

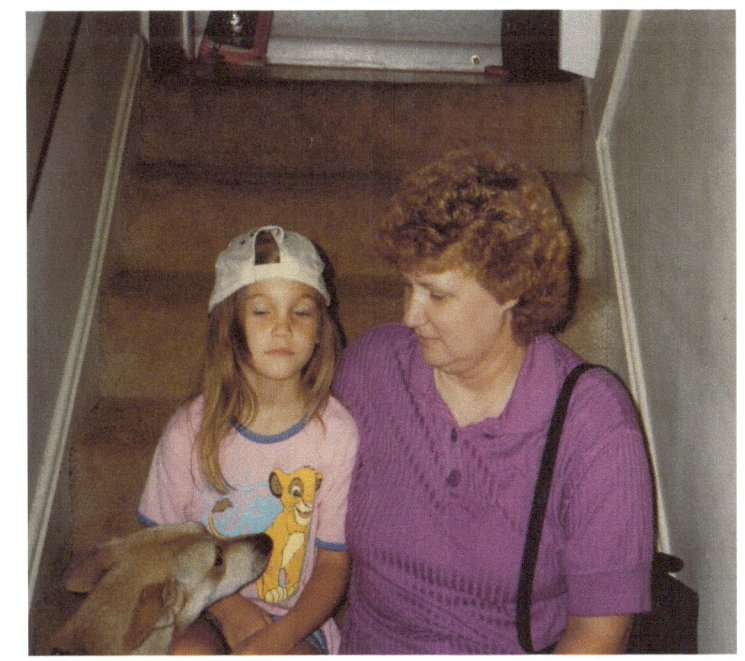

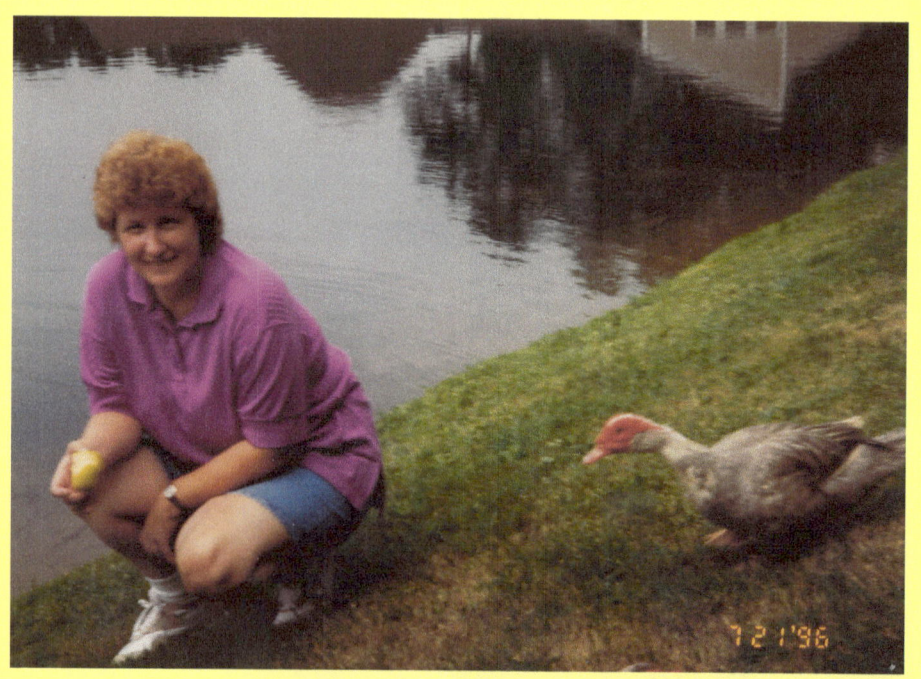

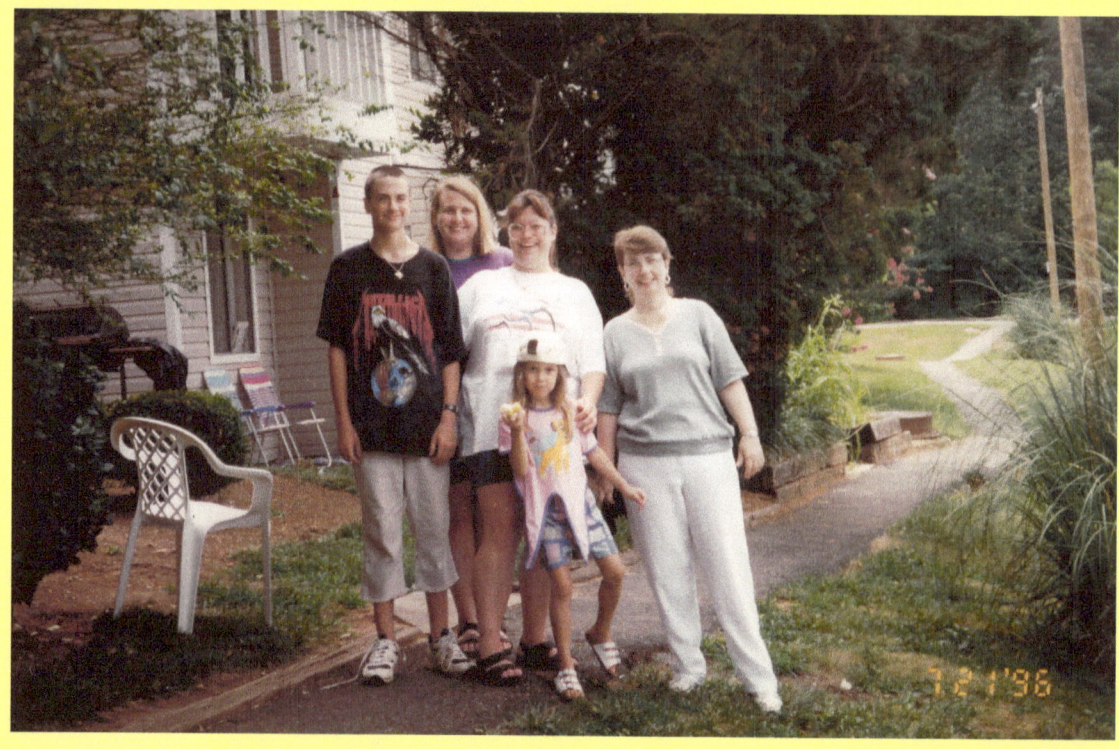

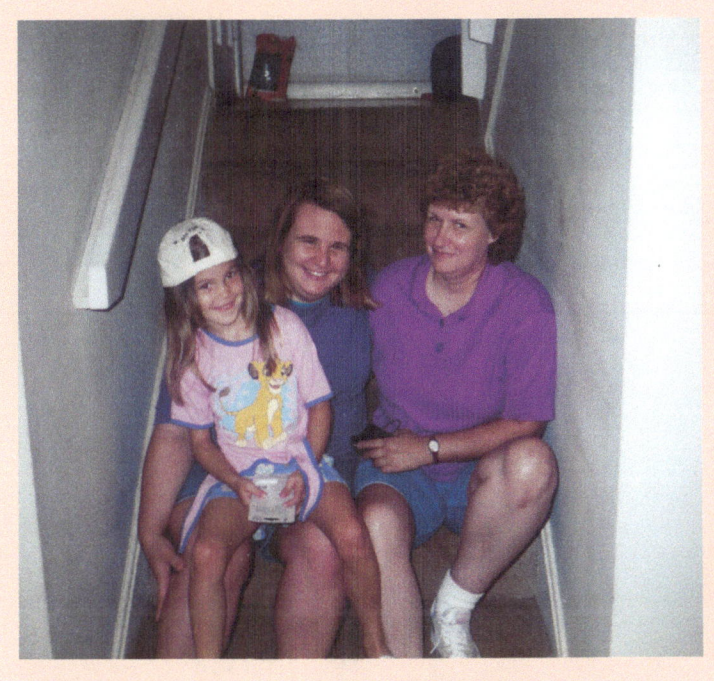

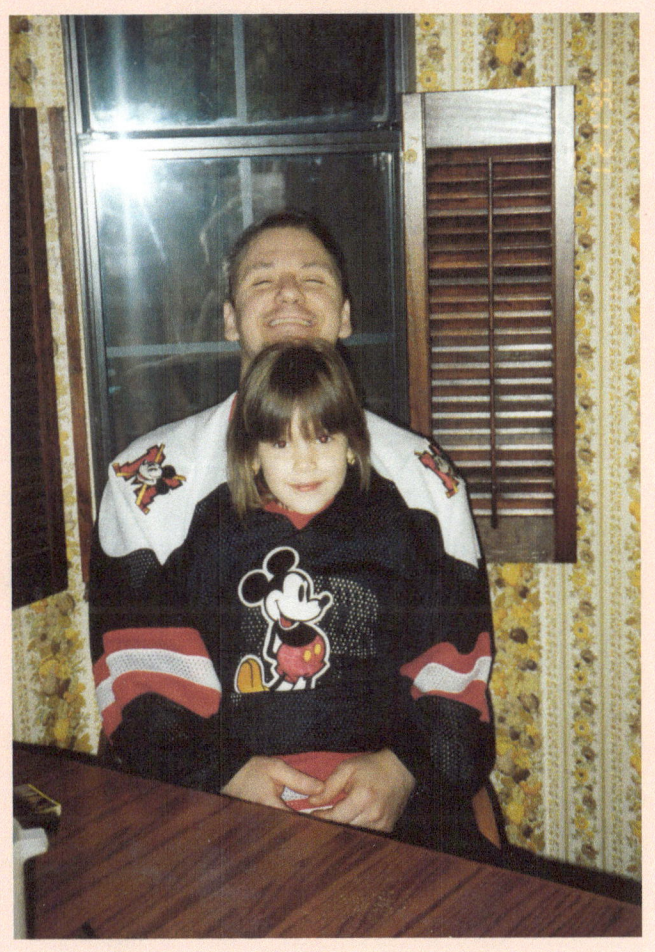

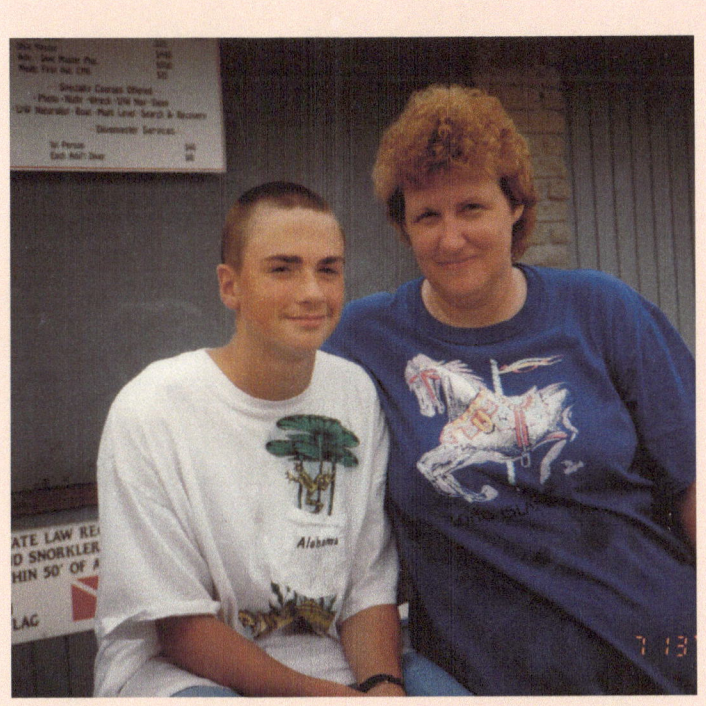

Family jokes, though rightly cursed by strangers, are the bond that keeps most families alive.

– Stella Benson

Rejoice with your family in the beautiful land of life!

– Albert Einstein

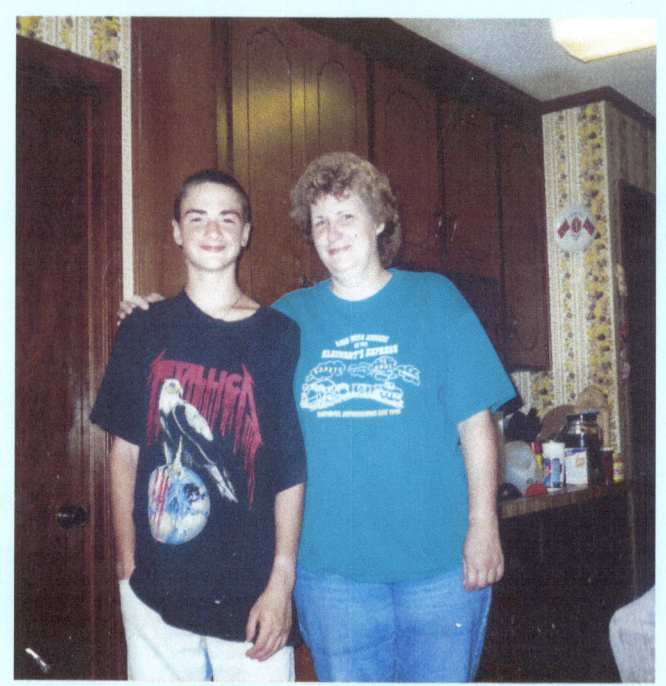

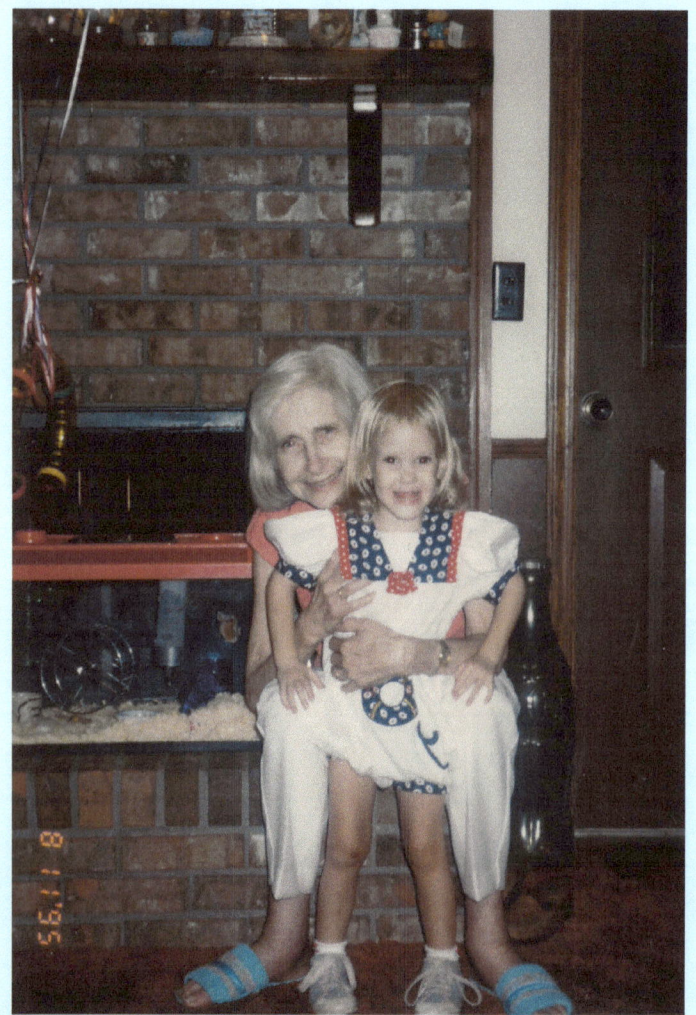

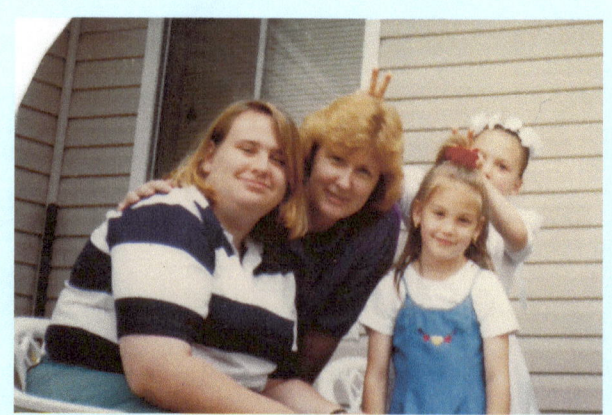

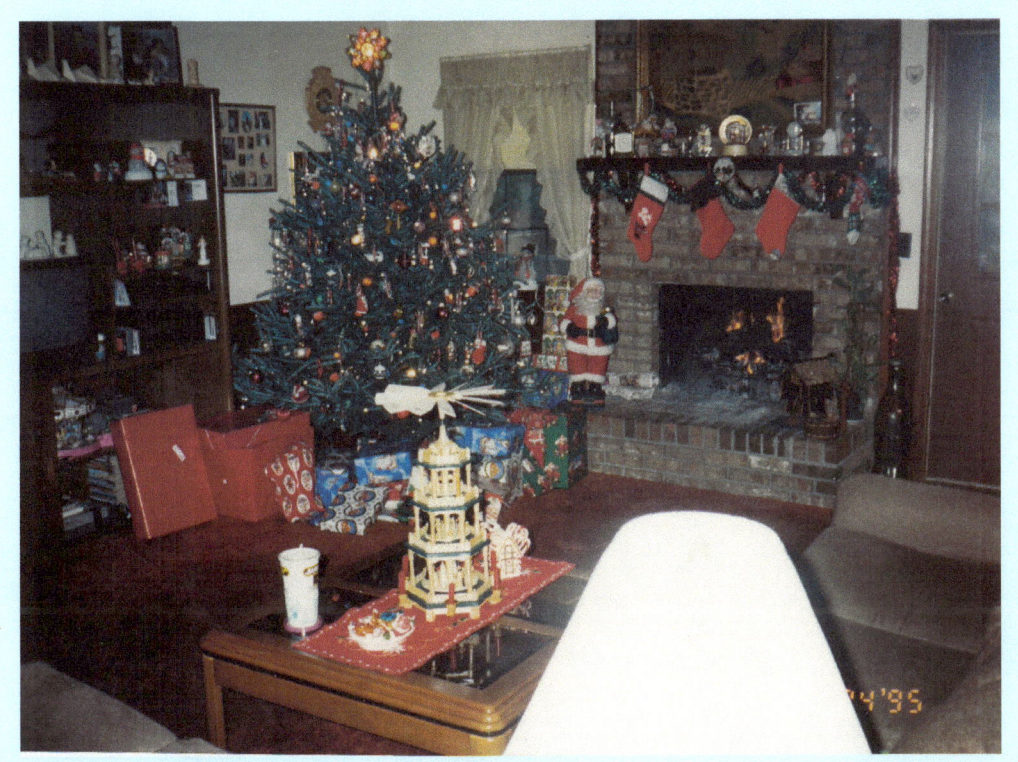

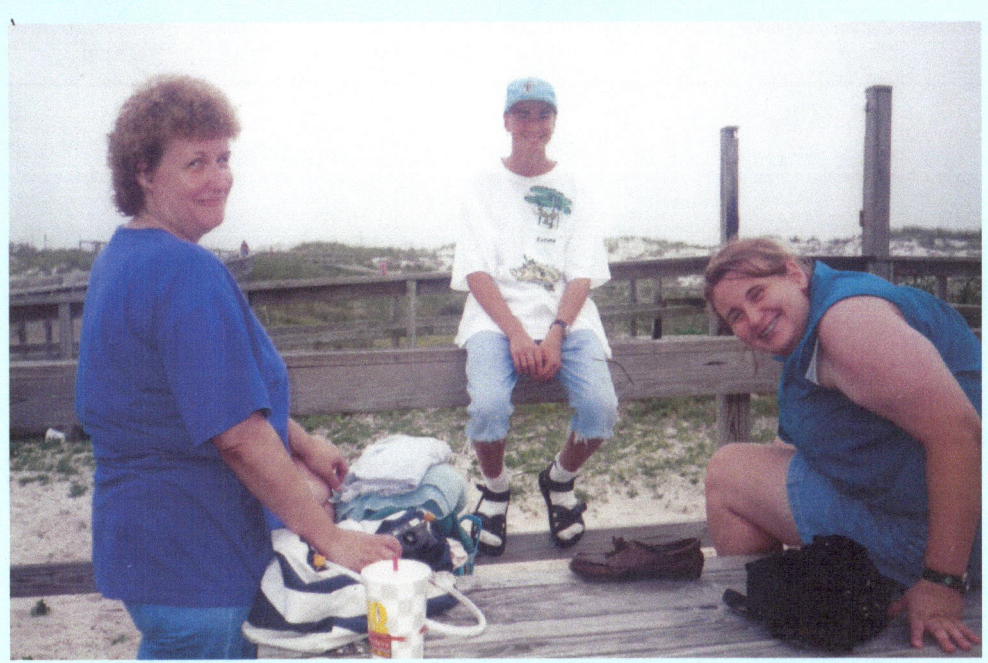

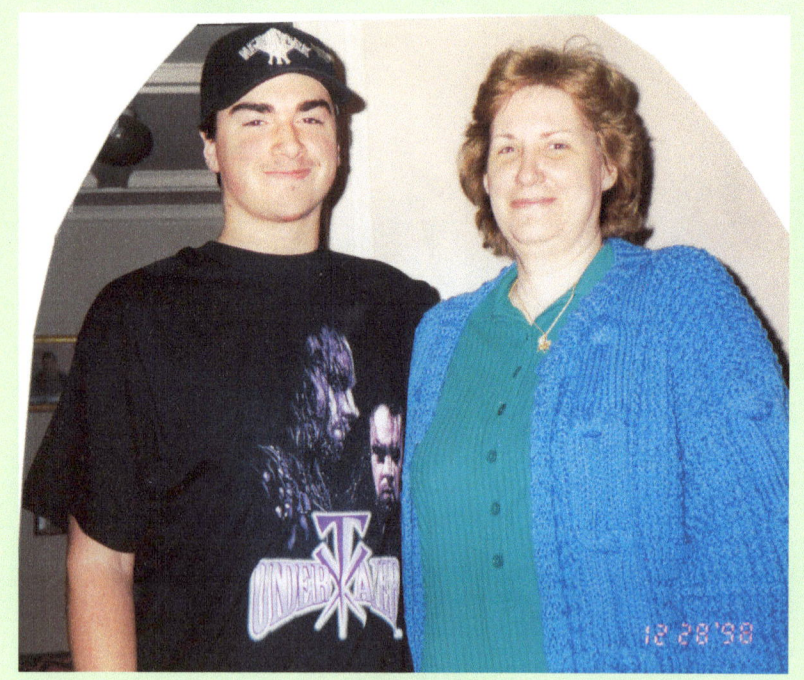

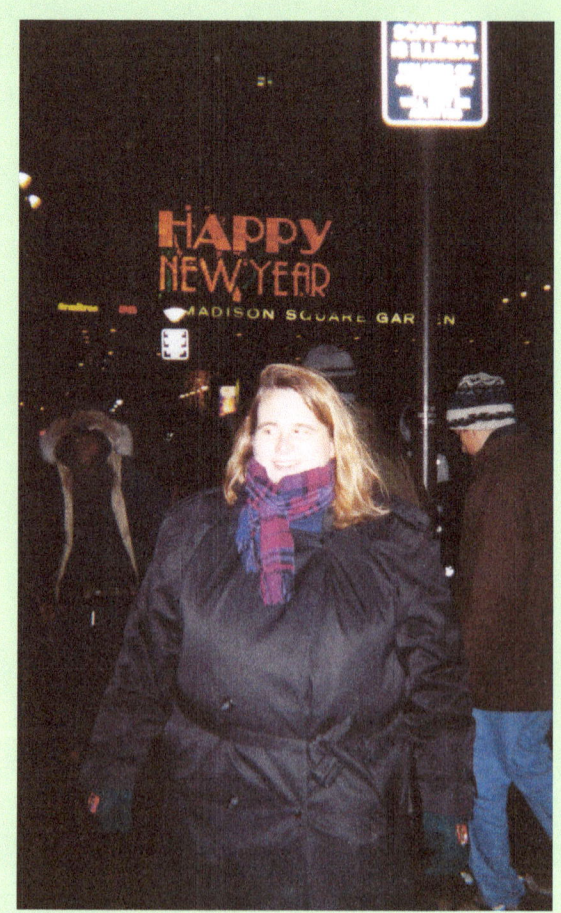

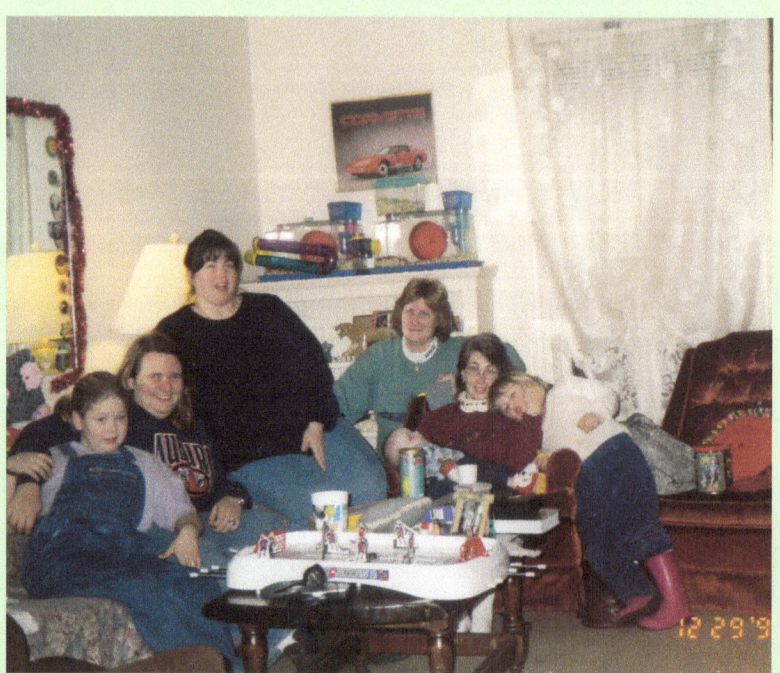

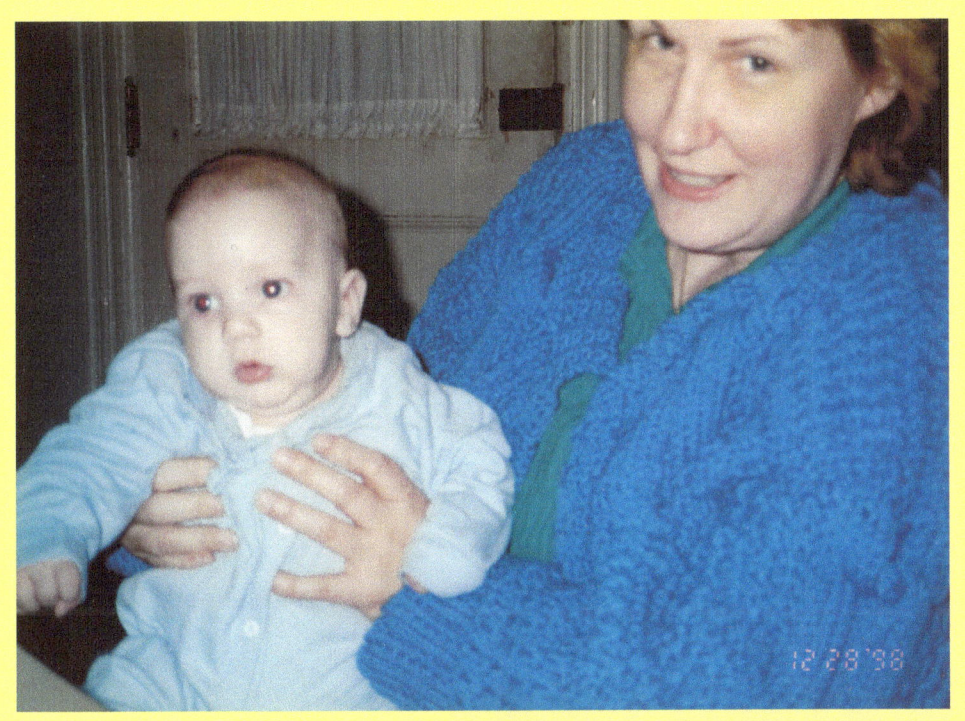

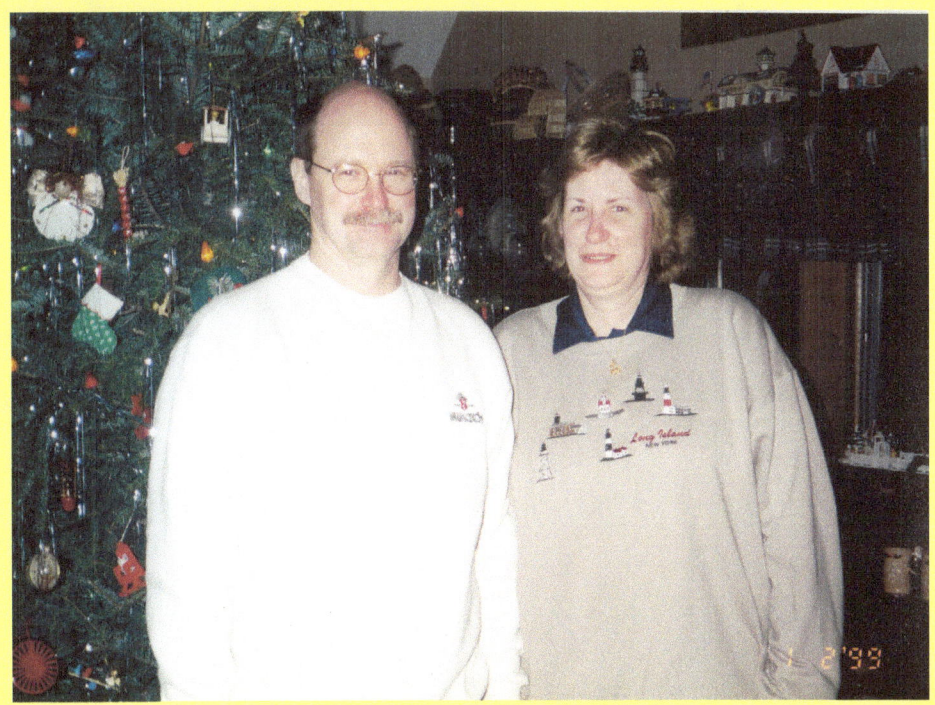

37

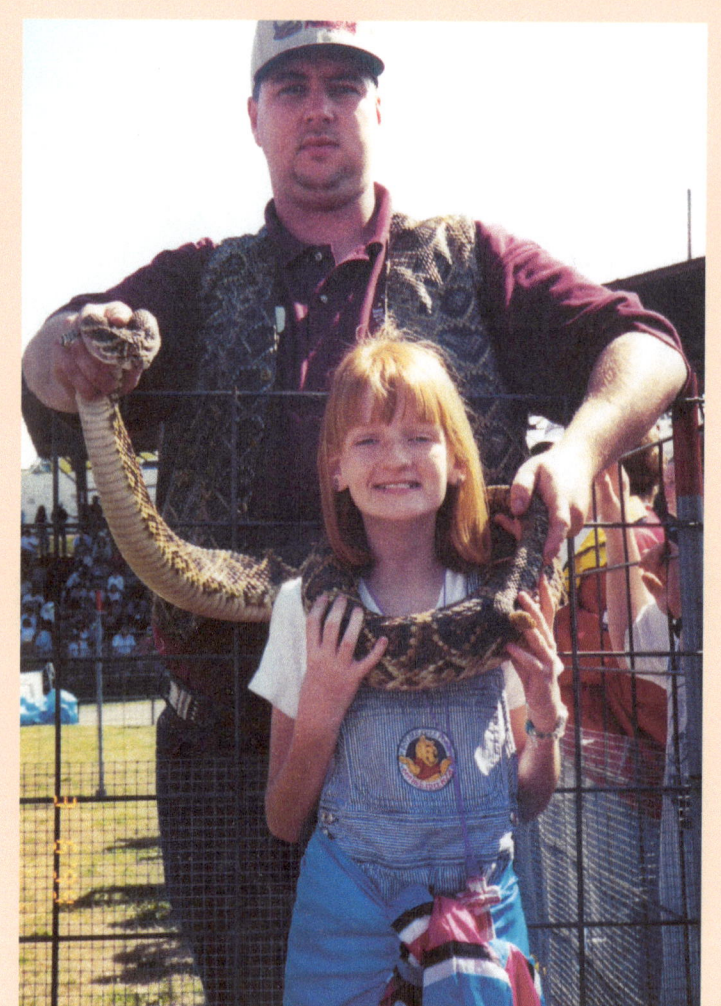

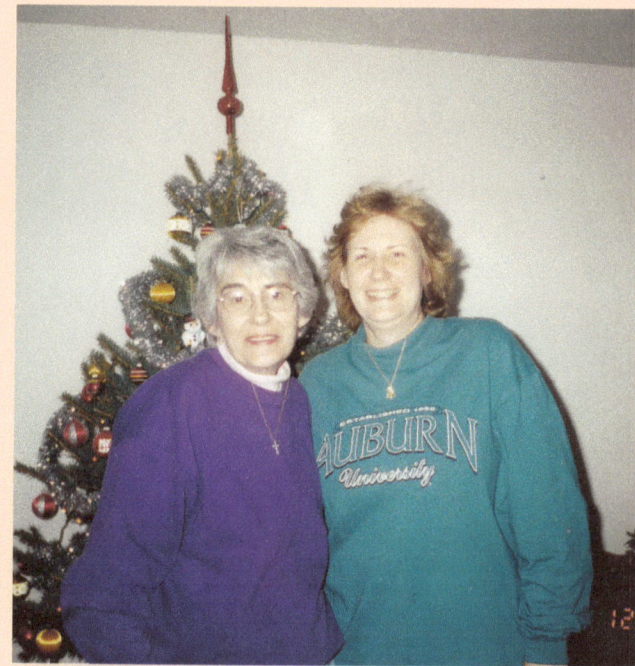

Family – where life begins and love never ends.

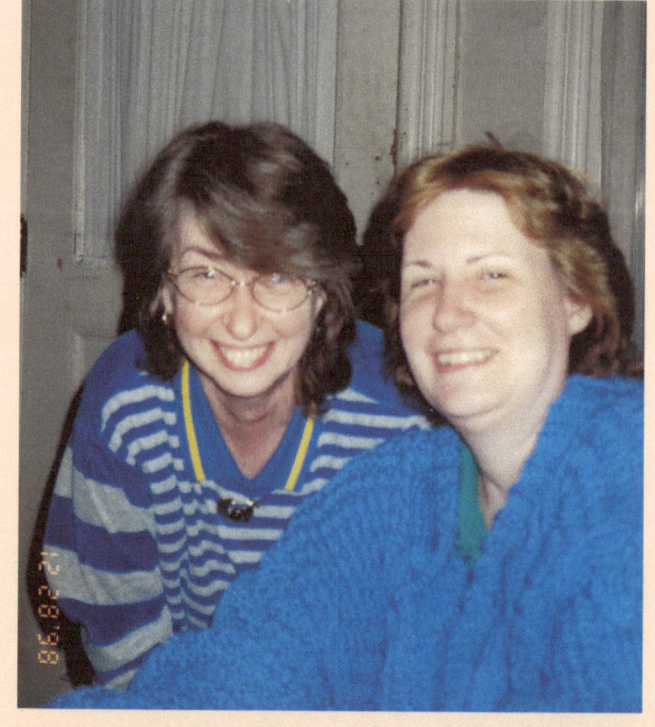

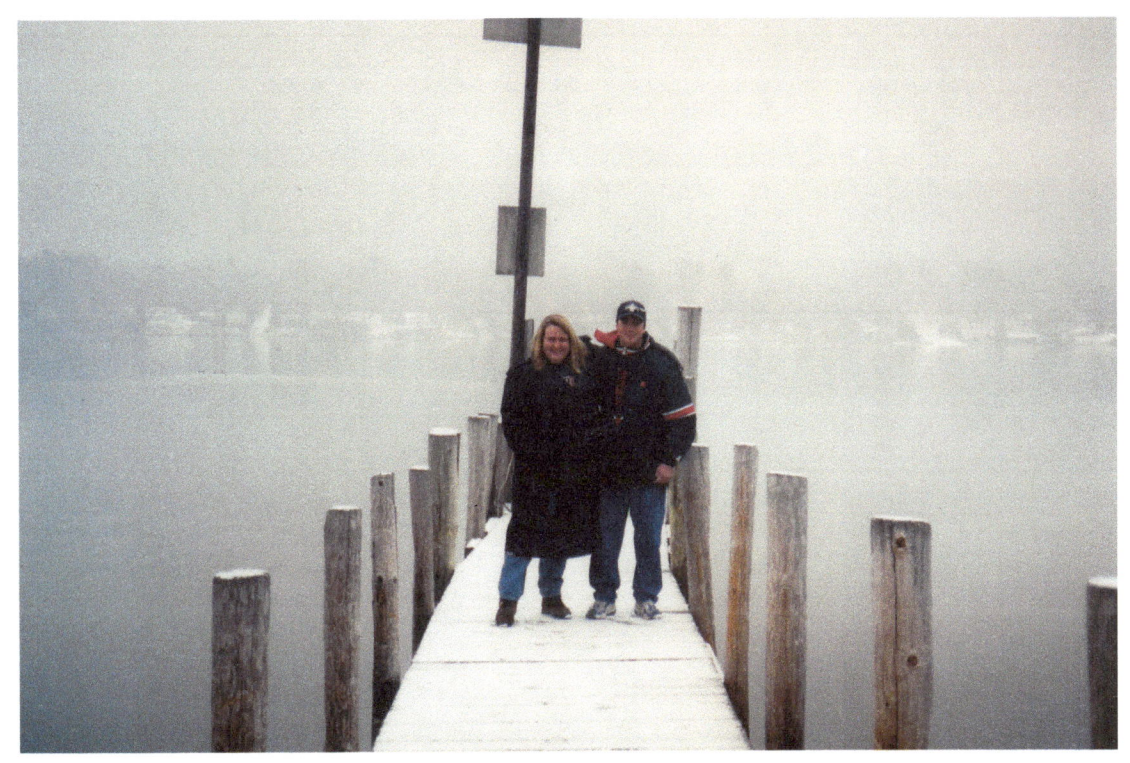

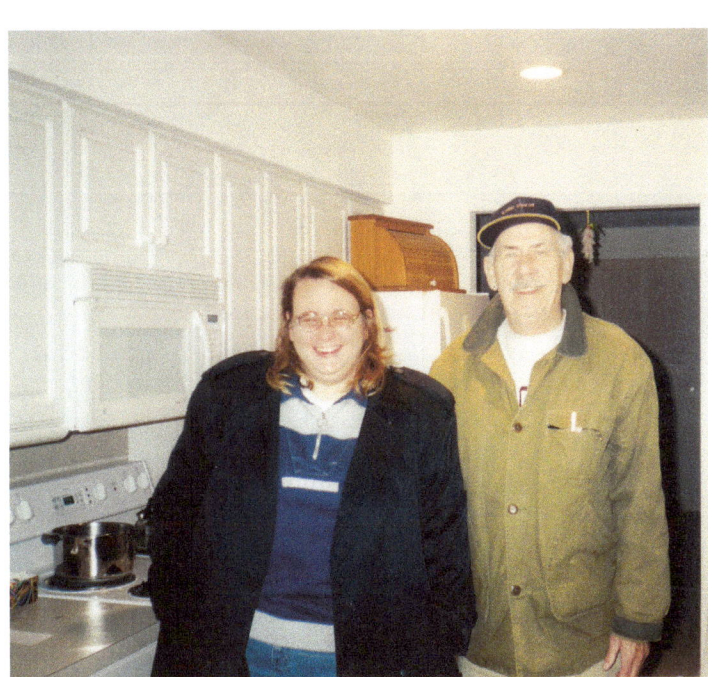

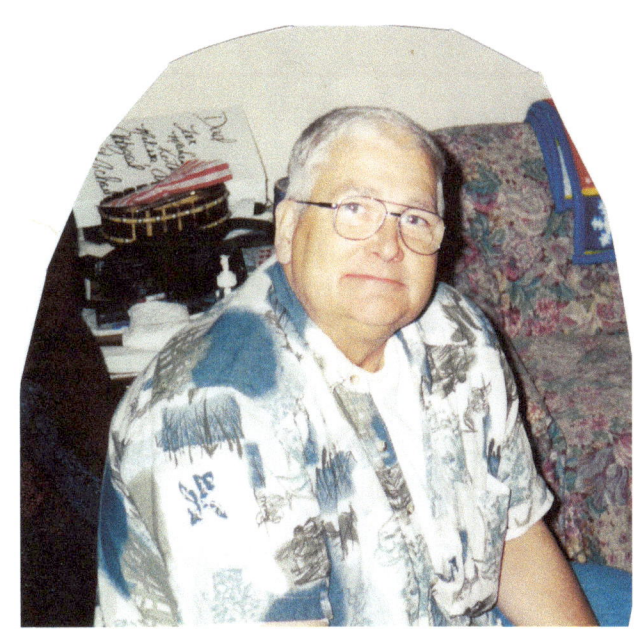

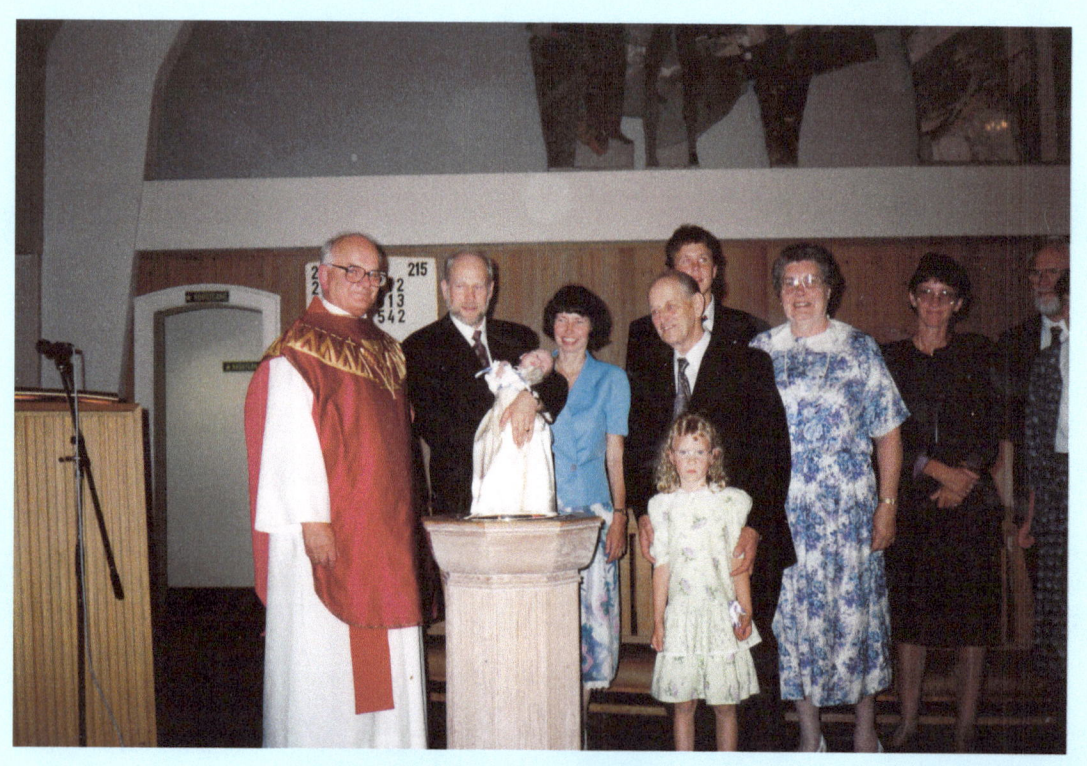

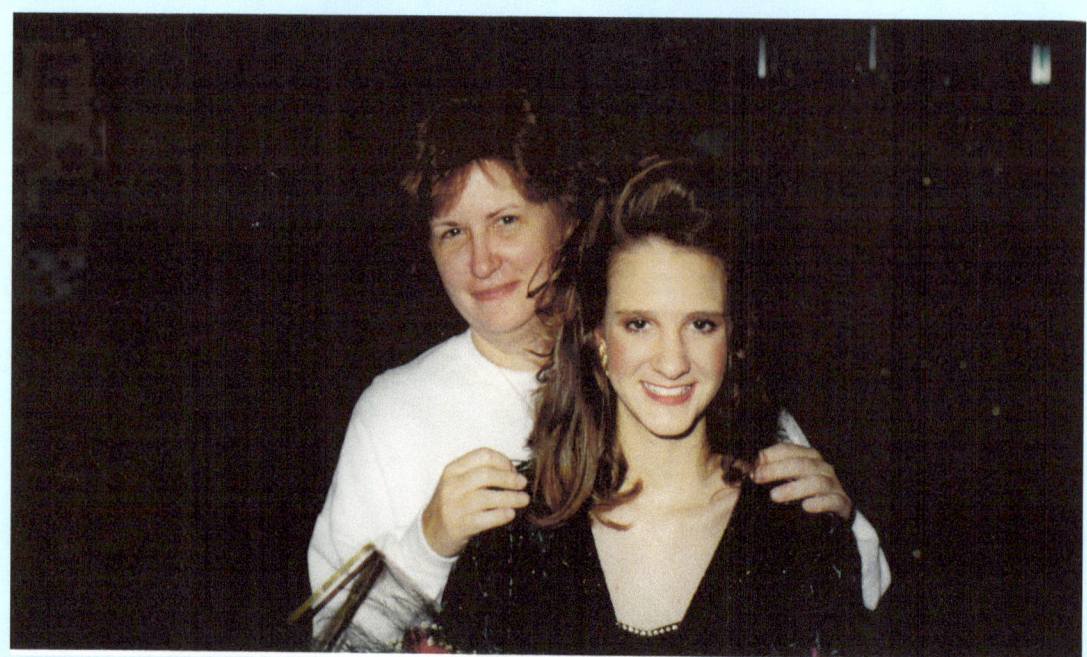

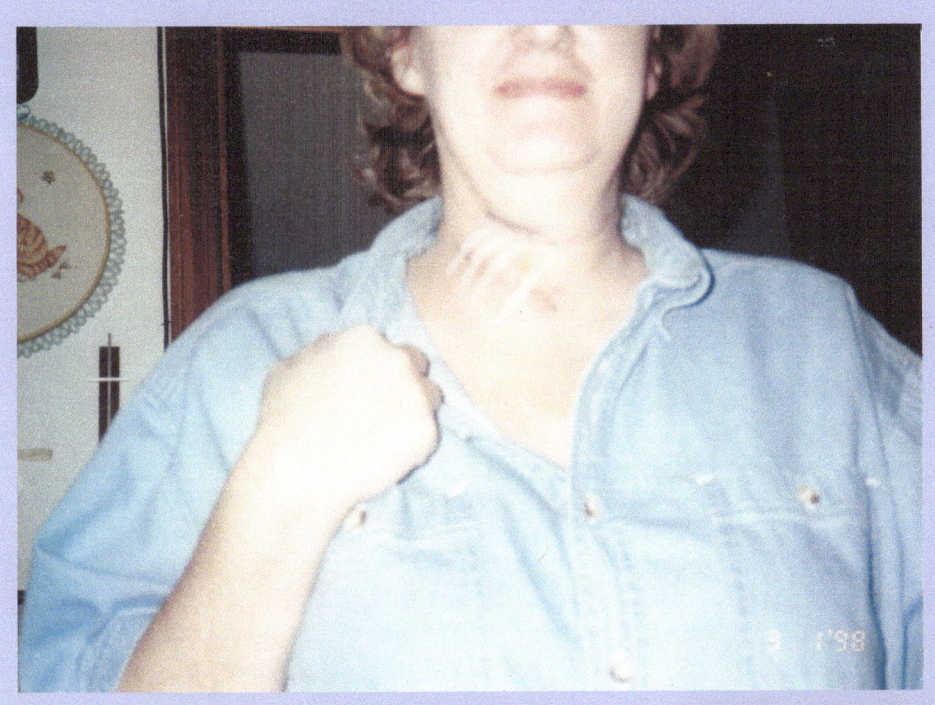

I know family comes first, but shouldn't that mean after breakfast?

– Jeff Lindsay

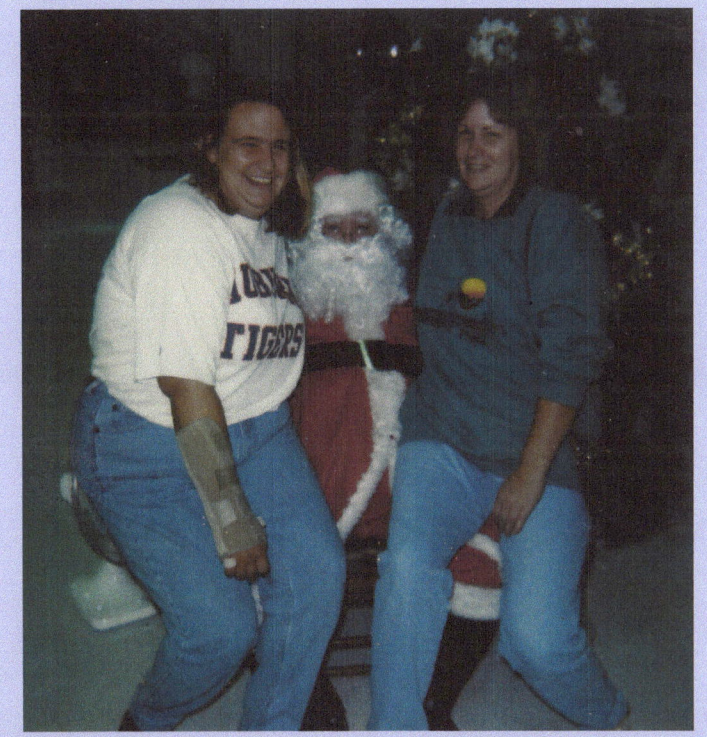

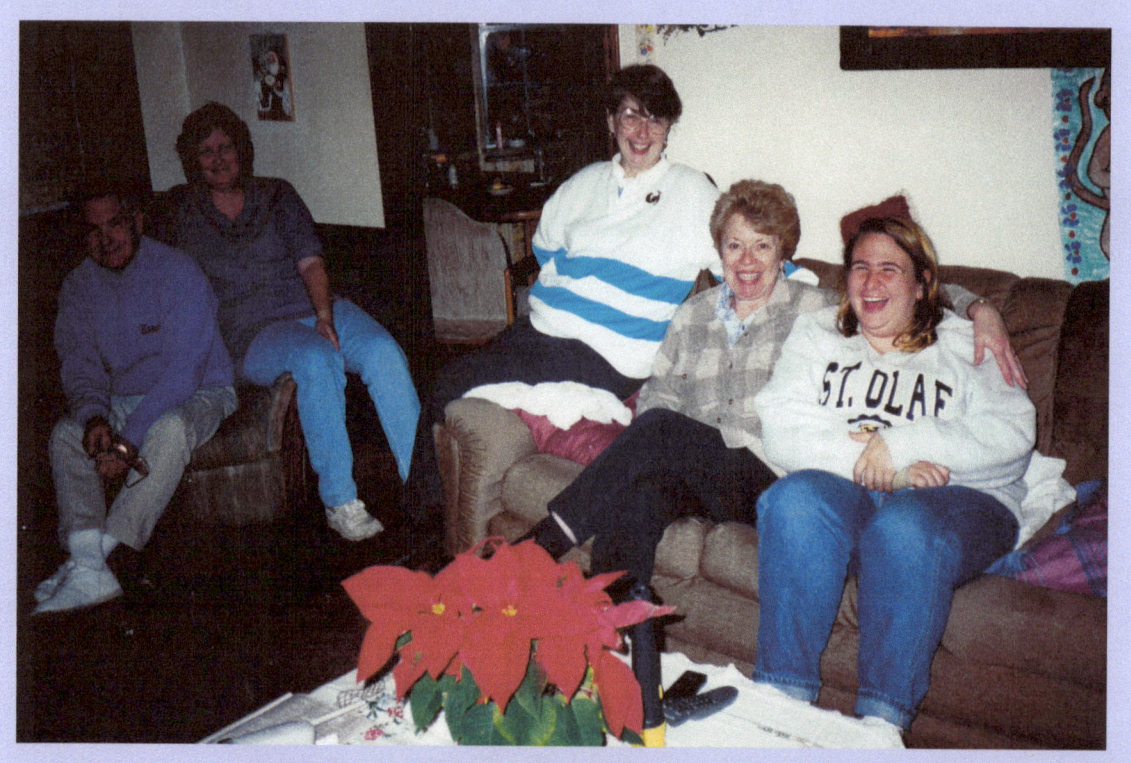

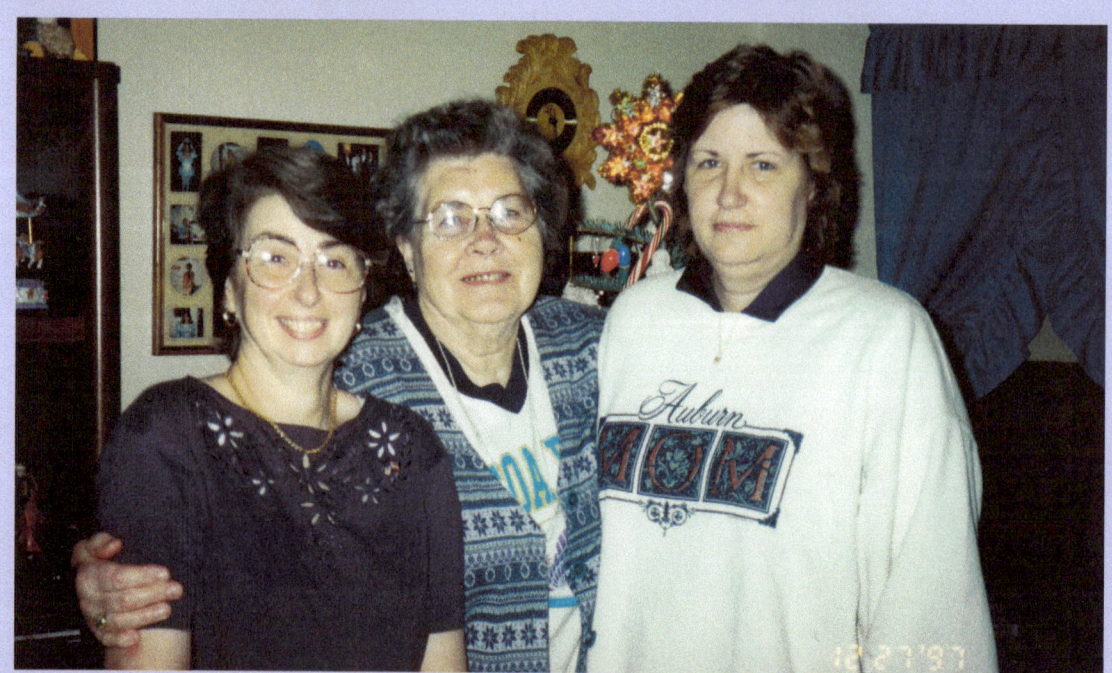

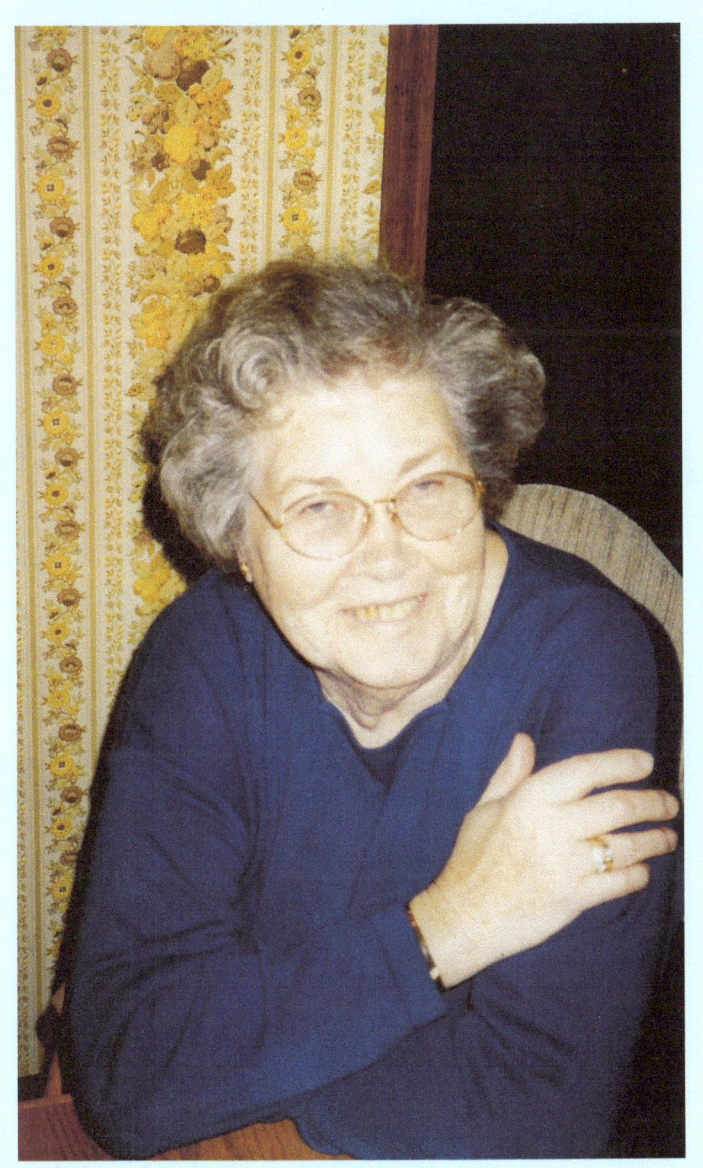

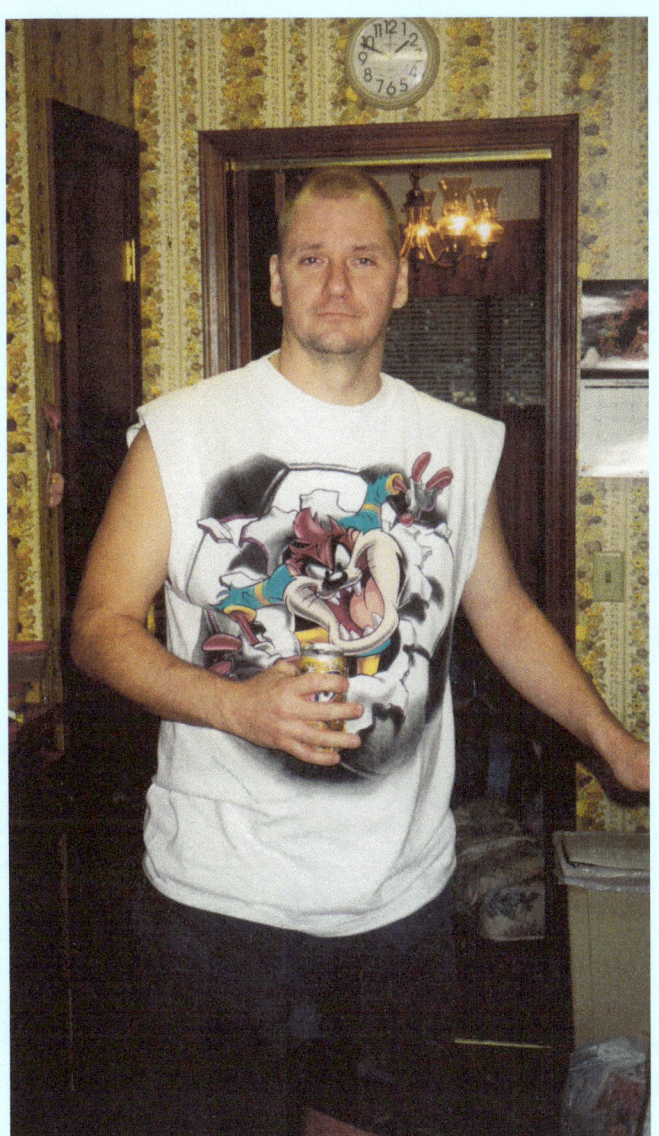

43

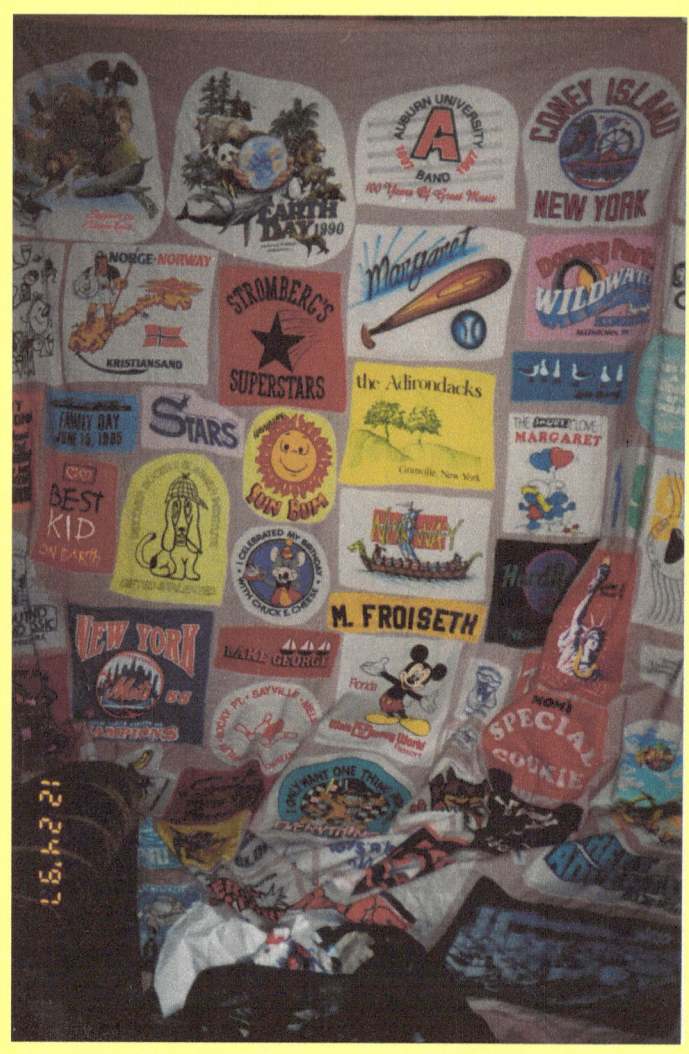

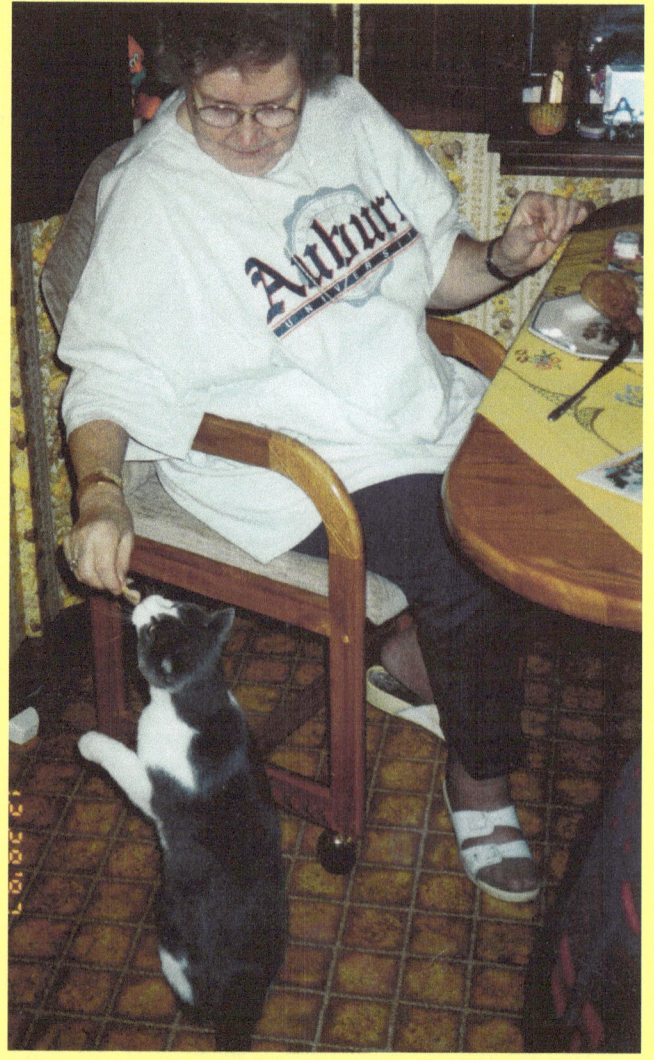

I would prefer to have no money but to have a nice family and good friends around.

— Li Na

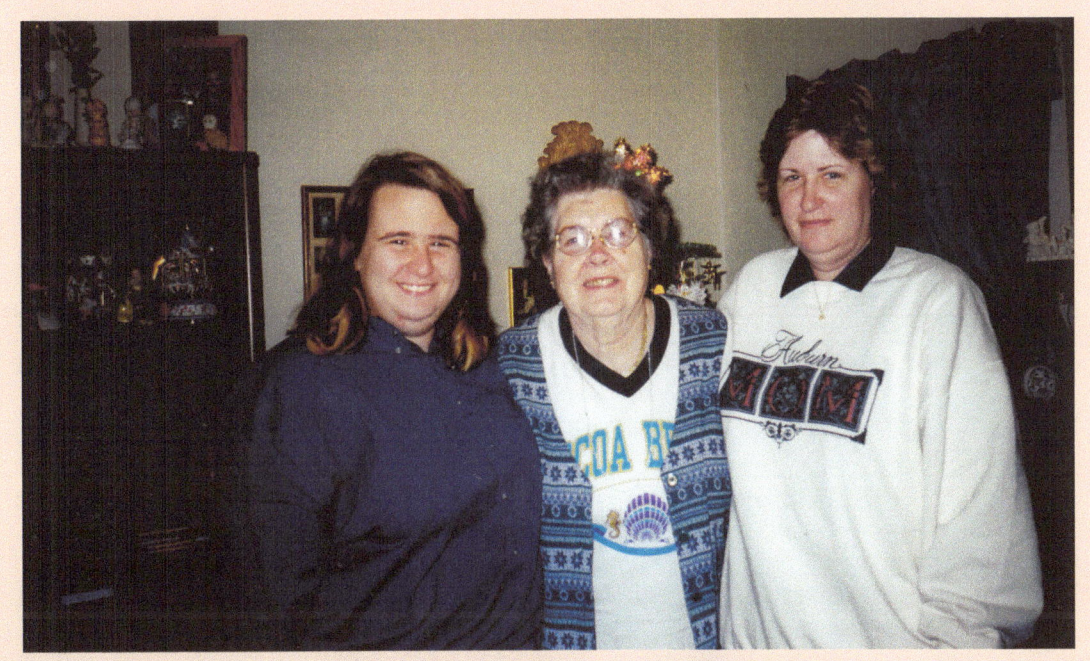

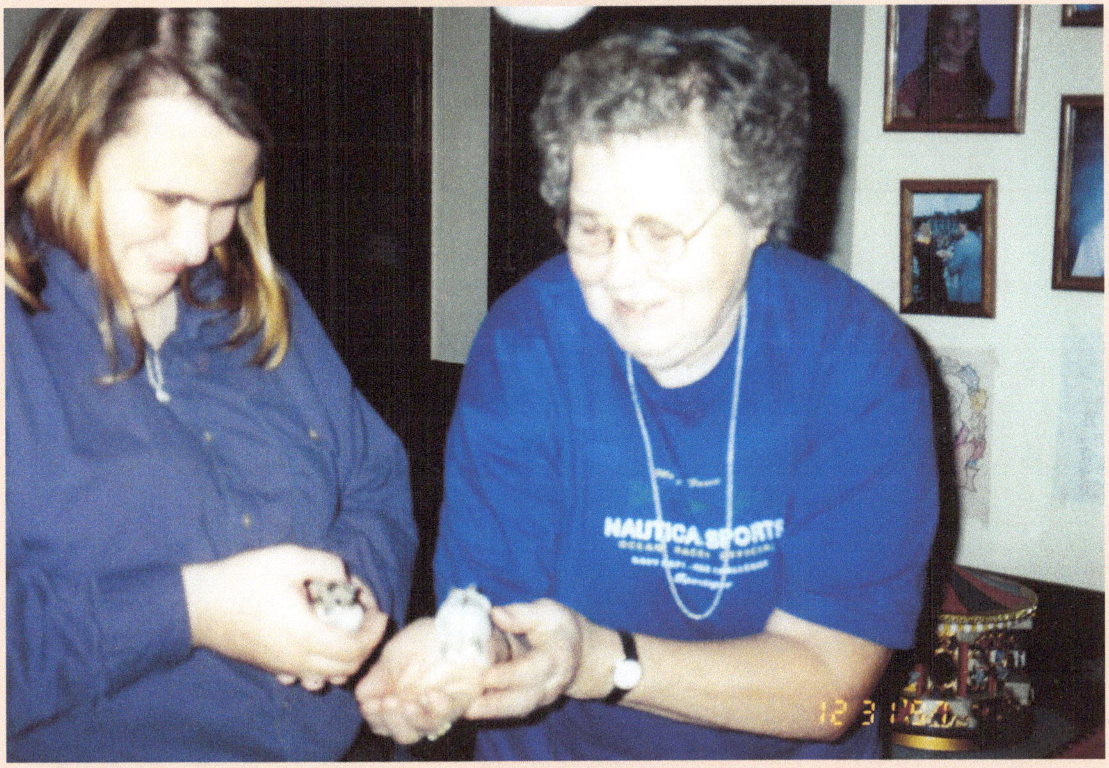

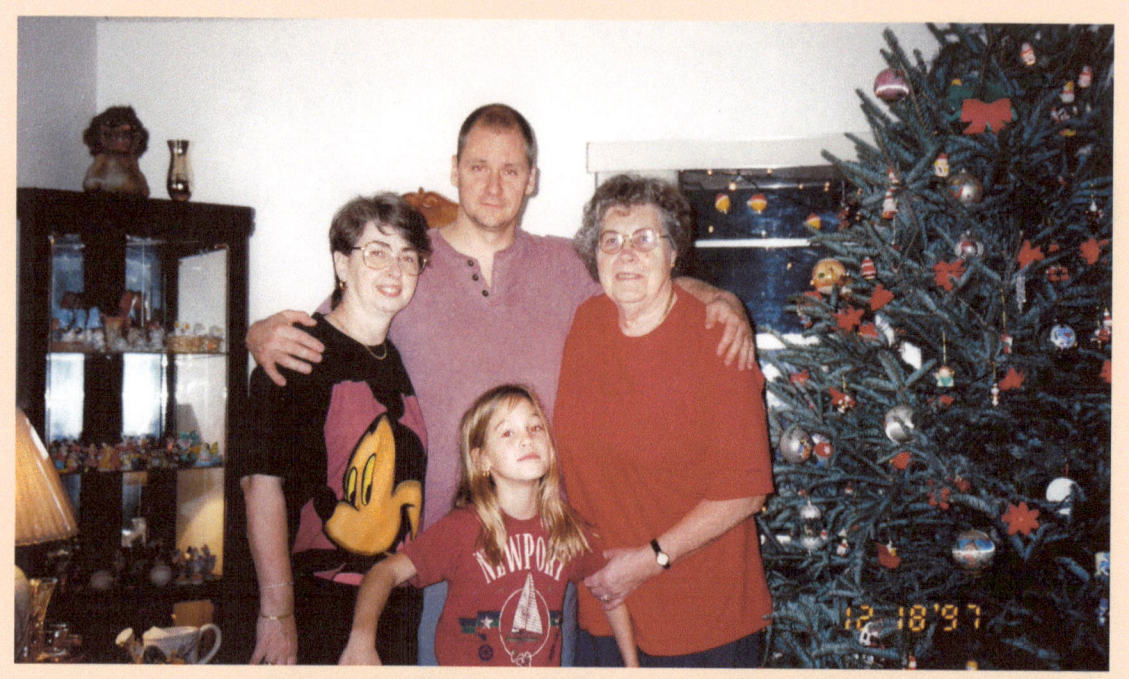

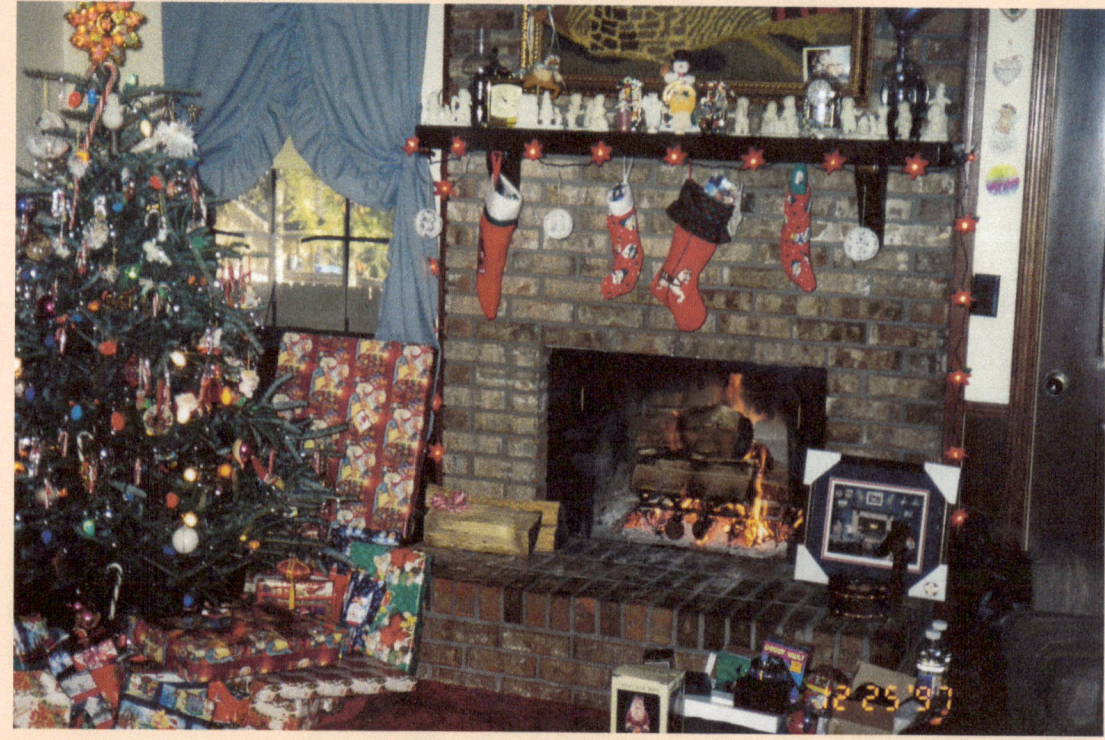

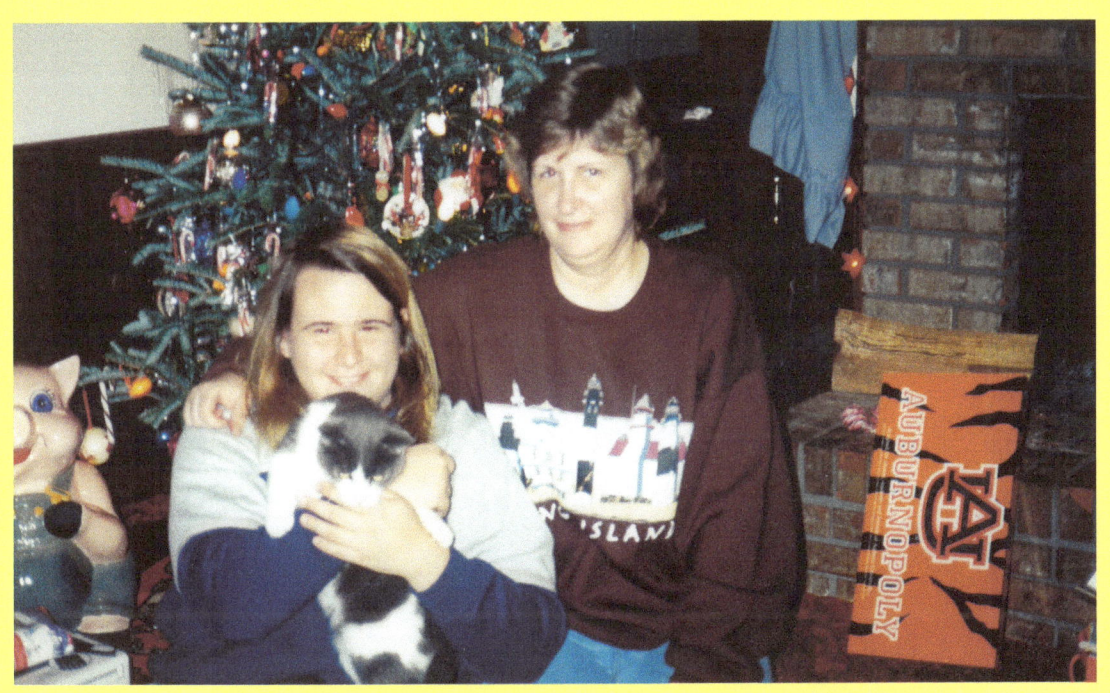

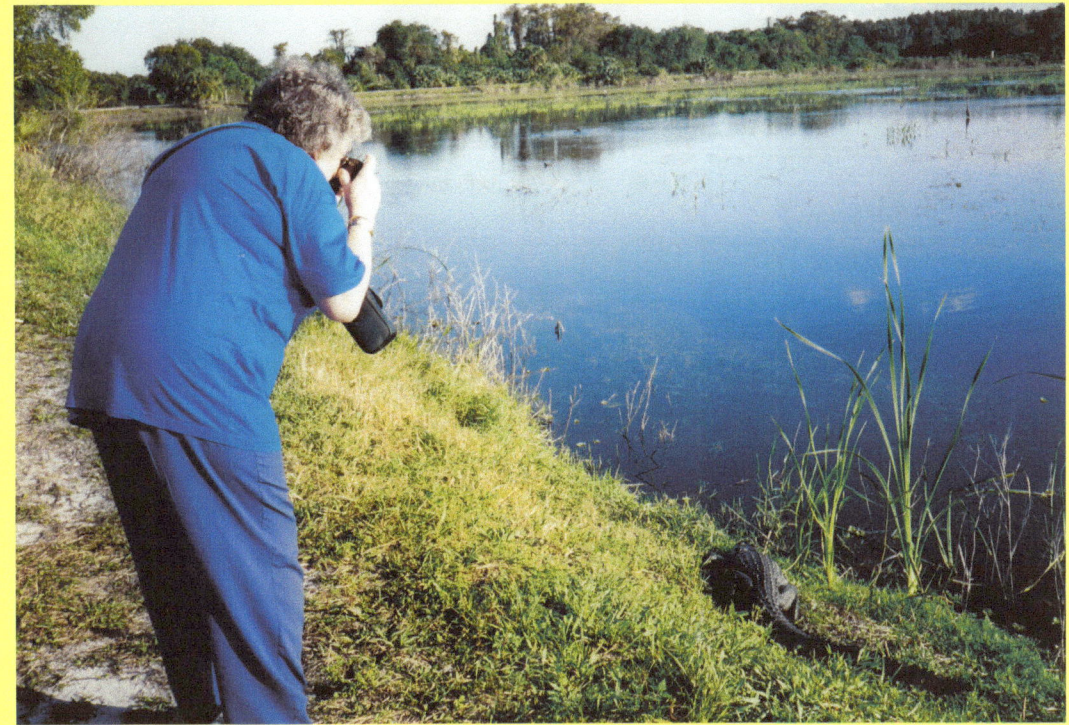

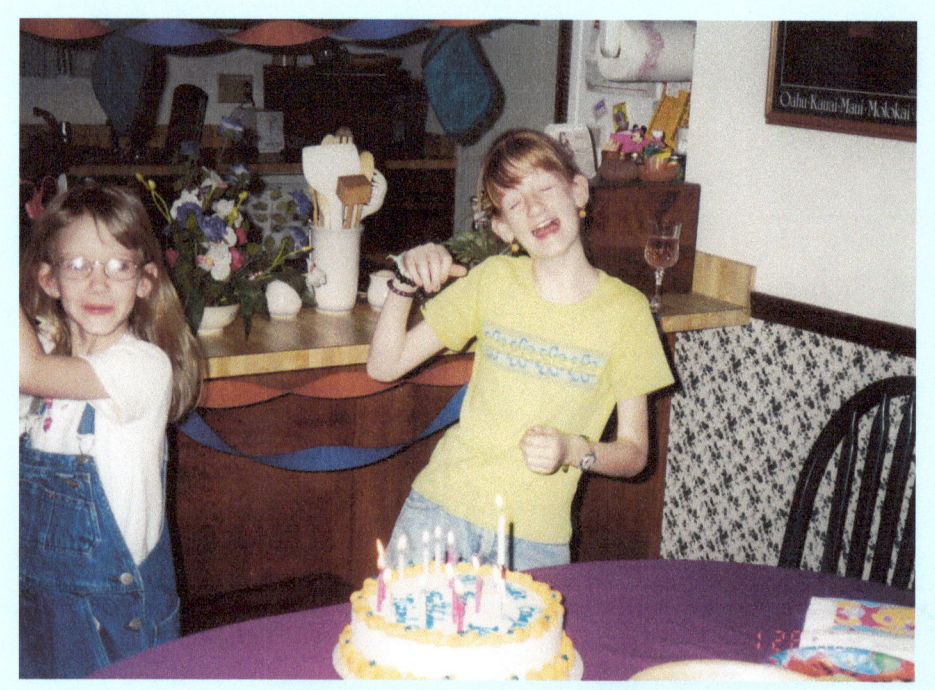

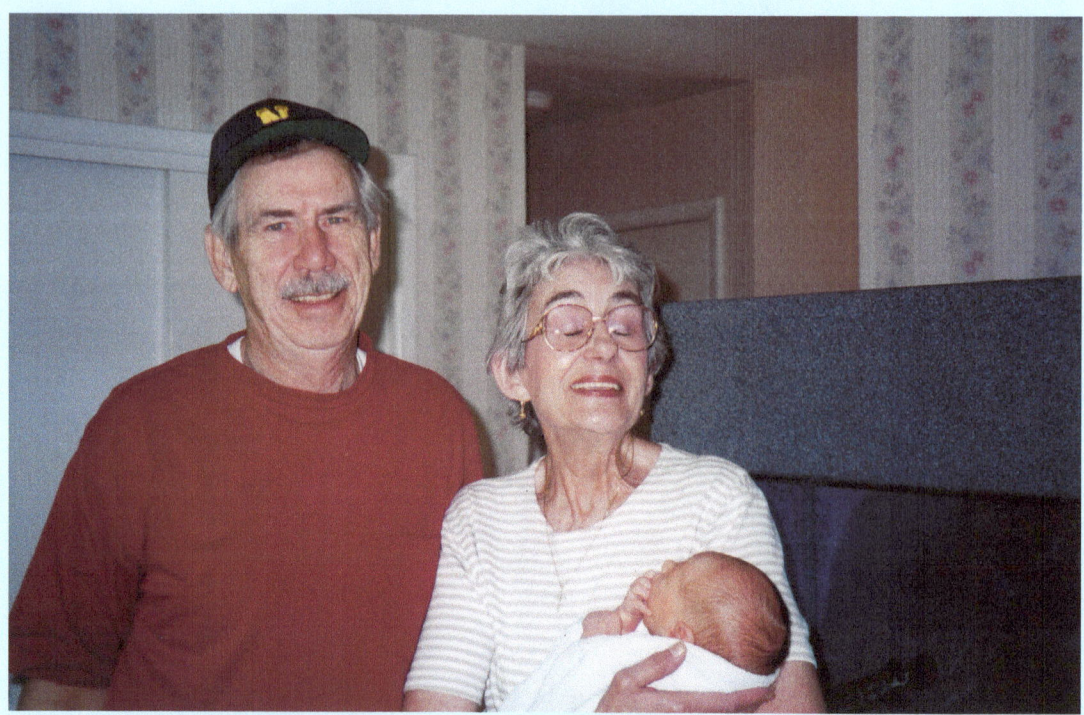

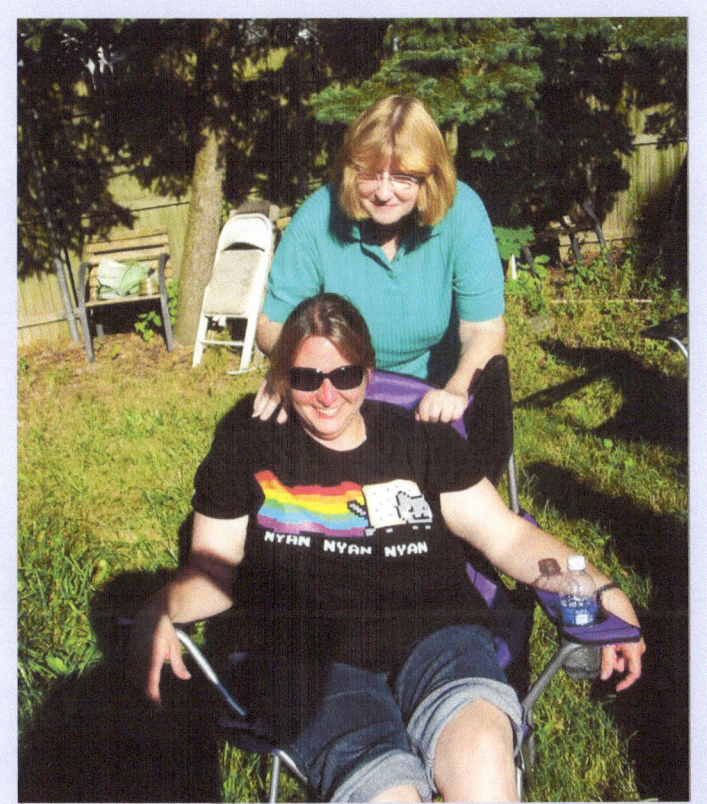

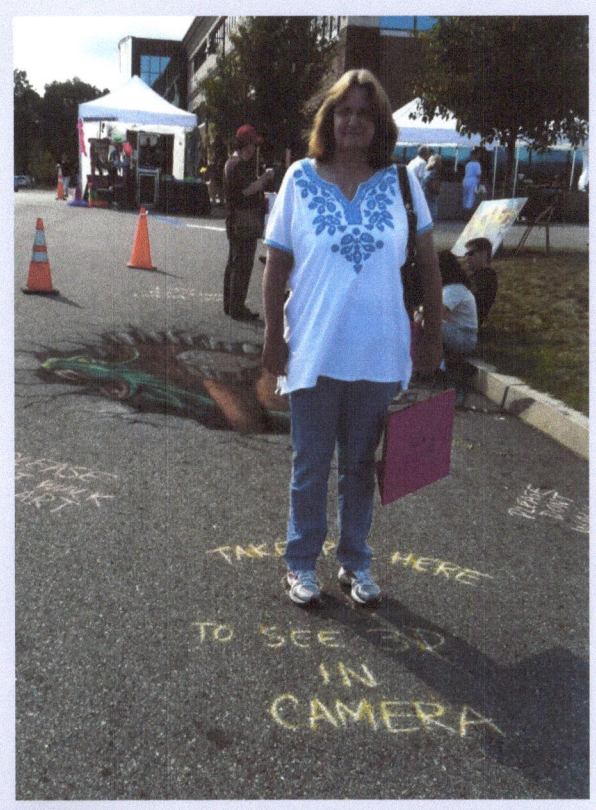

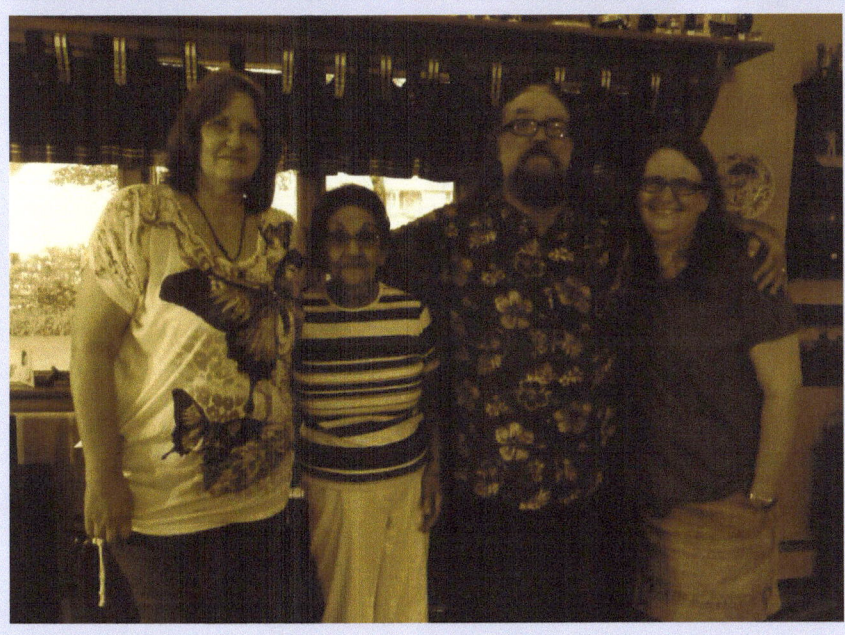

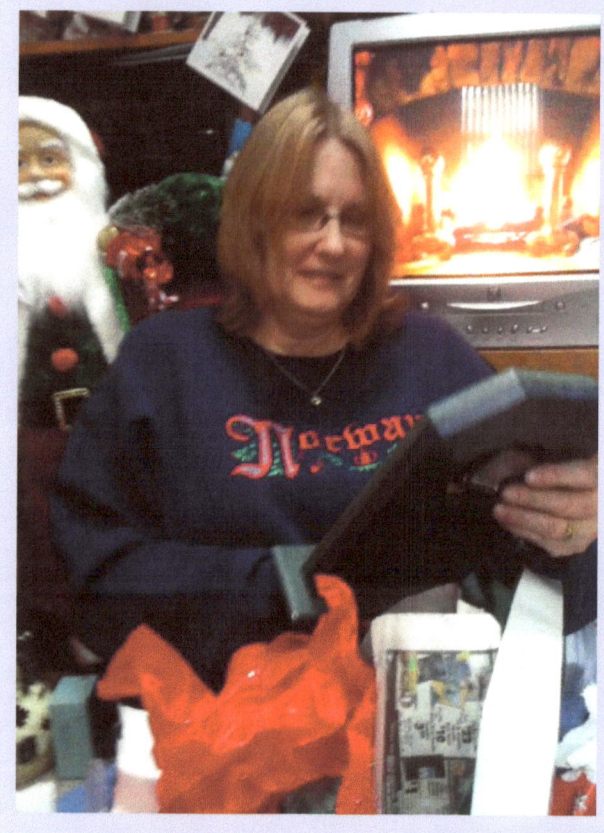

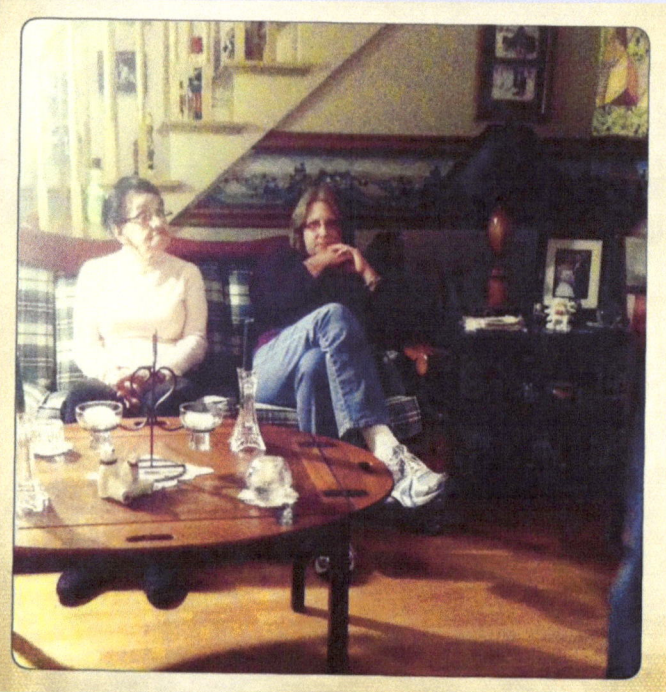

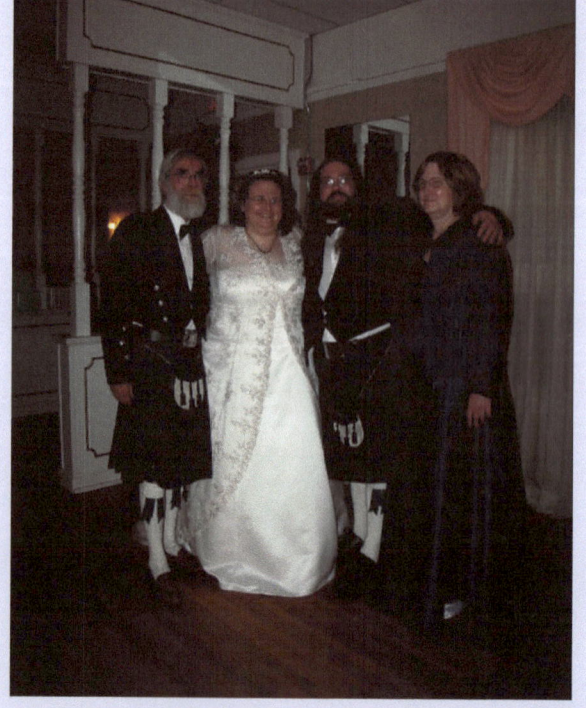

The family – that dear
octopus from whose
tentacles we never quite
escape, nor, in our
inmost hearts, ever quite
wish to.

— Dodie Smith

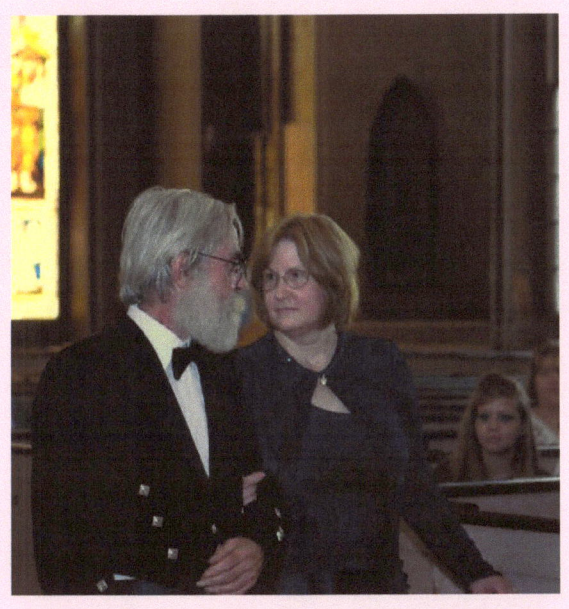

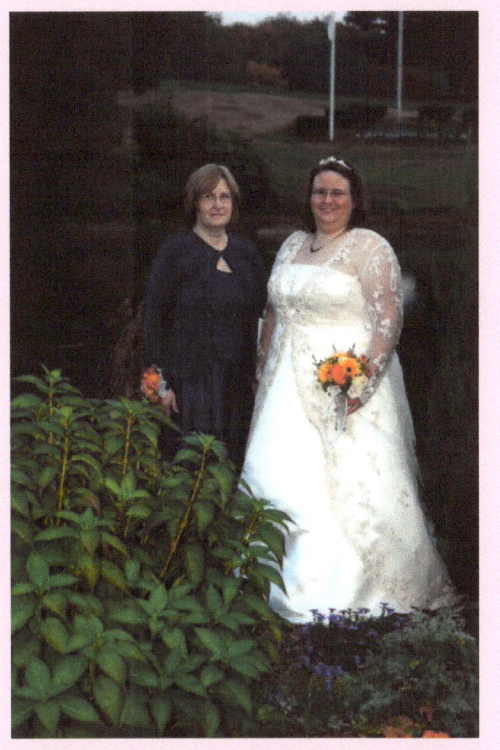

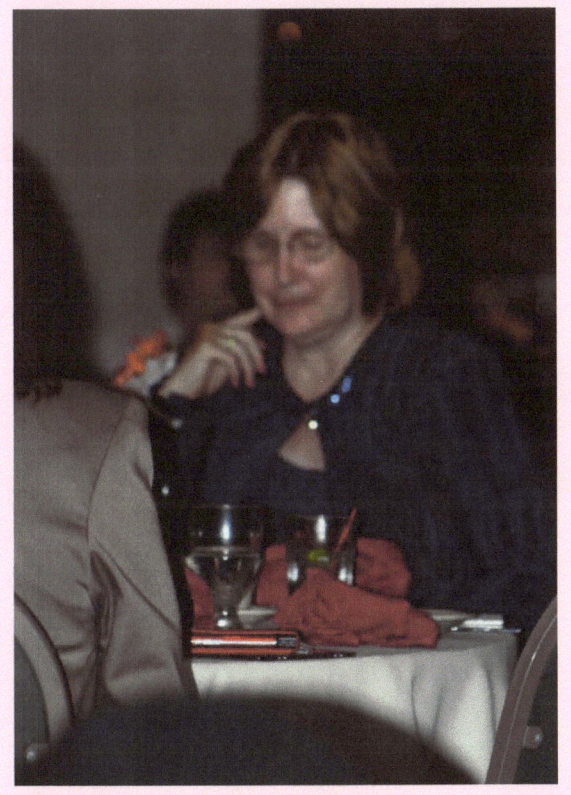

You are born into your family and your family is born into you. No returns. No exchanges.

– Elizabeth Berg

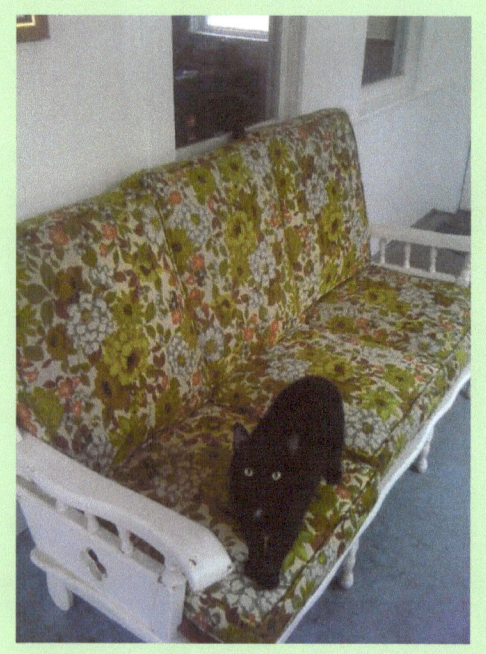

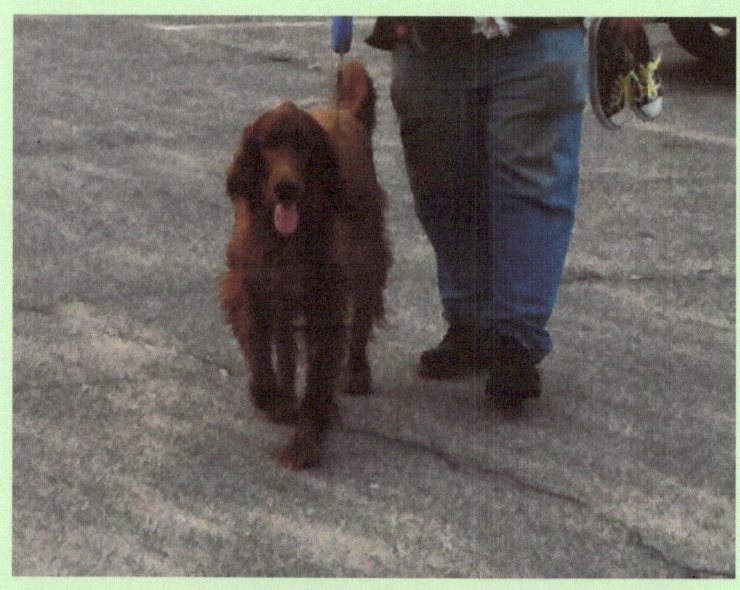

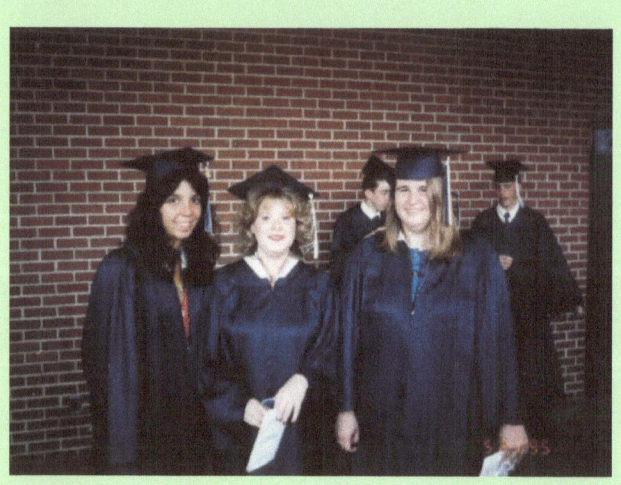

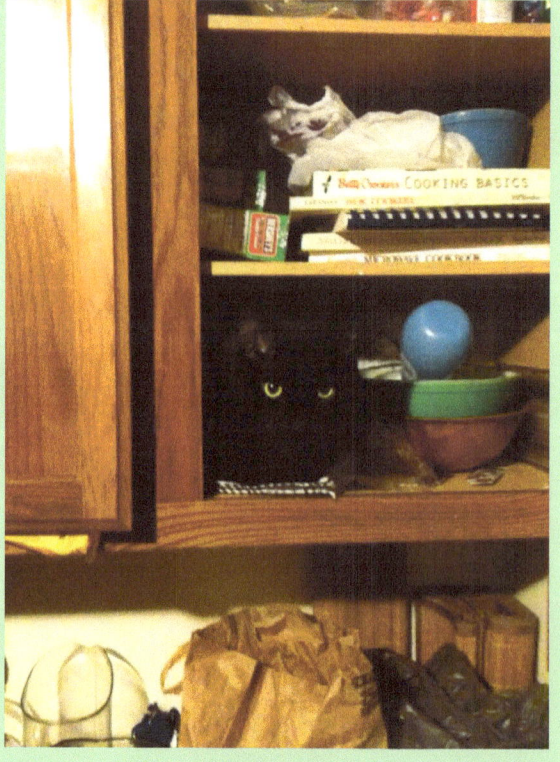

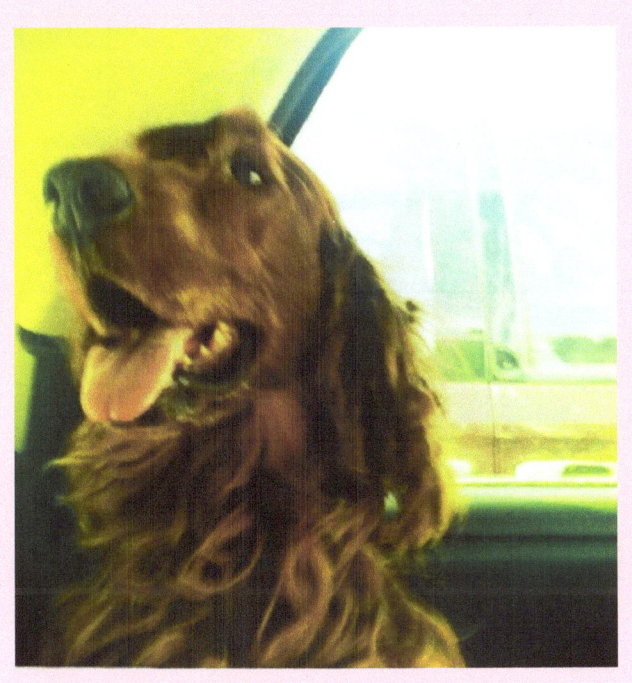

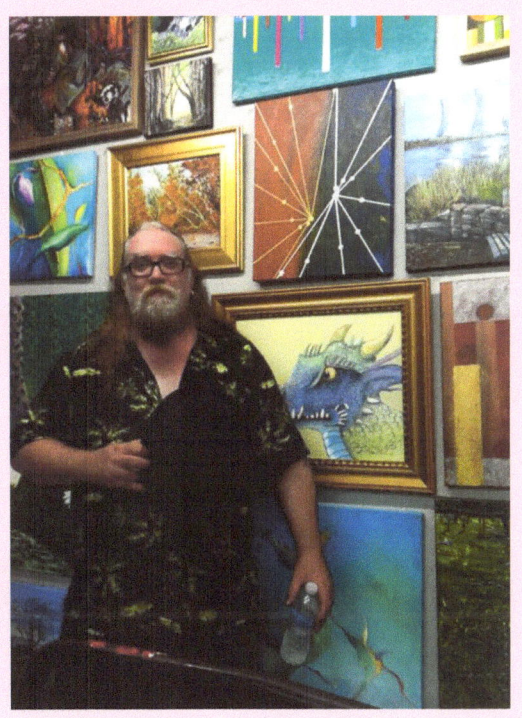

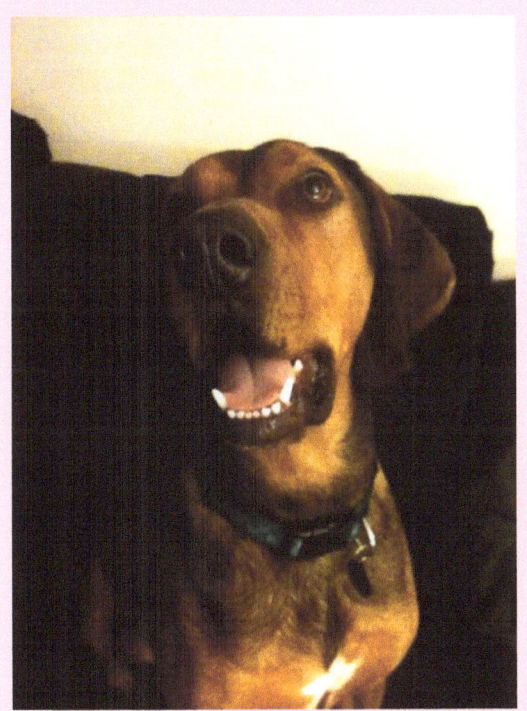

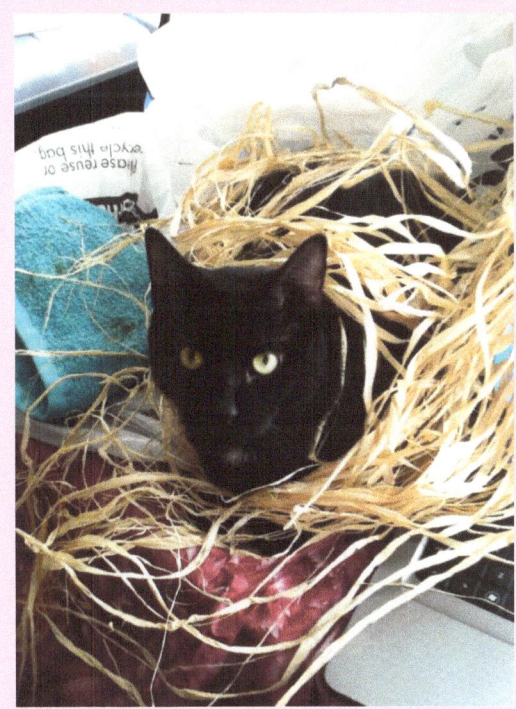

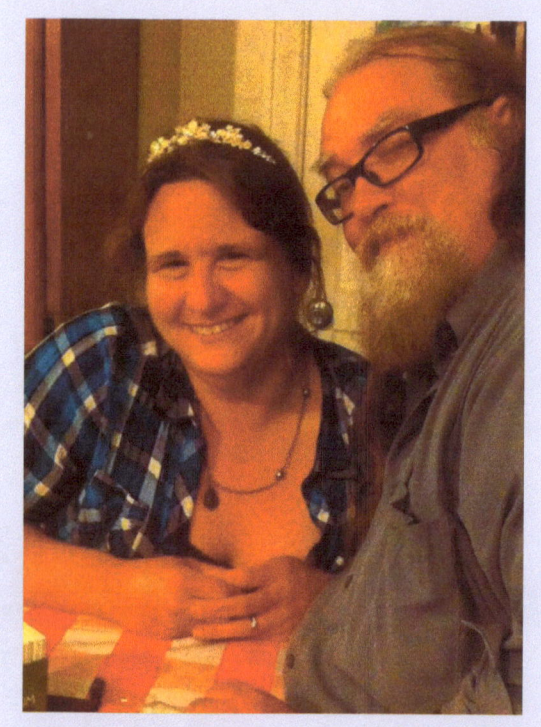

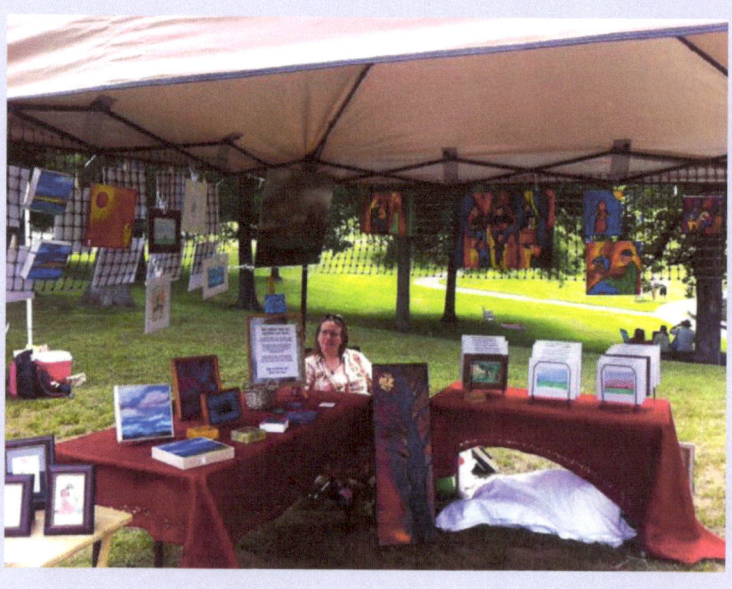

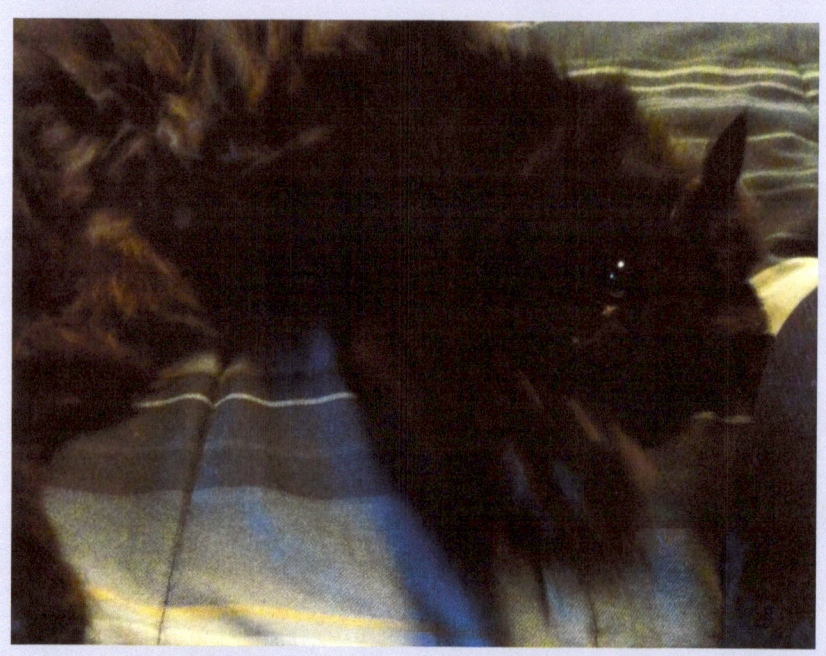

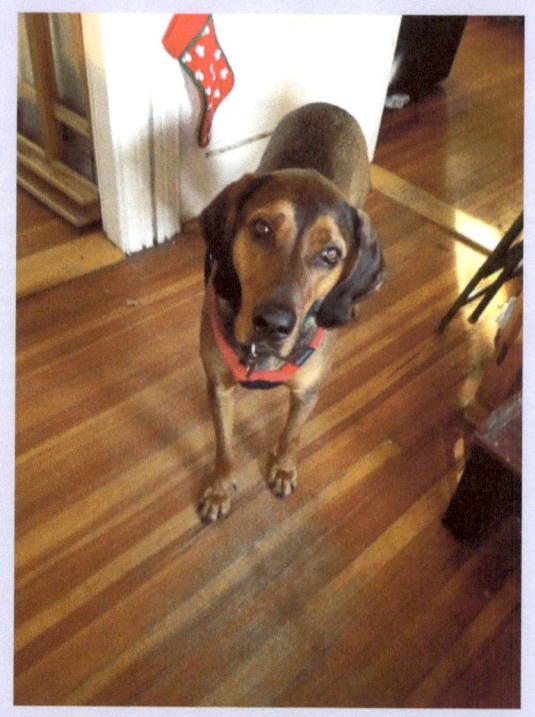

Aunt Lilly,

I wish that I knew where my photo albums were put in the storage unit because I would totally love to put a picture of your toe with this note! Some of my favorite memories from my childhood are visiting you in Alabama, those were some great summers and I will never forget going through all of the pictures that you sent in an album and at the very end was your gross toe picture. And the irony there is that now I look at my profession and when I see an athlete with bones sticking out or other great sports injuries I'm fascinated, so maybe you knew all along what I was supposed to do, lol. You are an incredible person and an even better Aunt and I am so thankful to have you in my life. I wish you many, many more birthdays! I love and miss you lots and lots!

– Candice

Dear Lil,

Wow, I can't believe that is has been 33 years since we met! To think I knew you & Margaret before I knew John too, lucky me! We've had some good times and bad but mostly great fun! I remember Eric getting you a Primed, Black VW Beetle and teaching you how to drive standard shift from the passenger seat. Remember the heat never shut off either? I was so honored to have you as my Maid of Honor when I joined the family. Your moving away was tough but we knew you did it for the right reasons, but that never stopped us from seeing each other often so we aren't going to stop bugging you till we get it right and we are in the same state again LOL! At least we have phones where the conversations just keep going, we never run out of things to say. NYC is always going to be fun whenever we go back—from a Simon & Garfunkel concert, to China Town for Coach bags to the World Trade Center at Ground Zero sharing with Brittany (who tried to teach you how to text on the train, thank goodness you finally caught on). I wish that I could be there for your "40th" year young birthday but a contractual commitment won't allow it. Too bad your birthday wasn't on a different date! Hopefully we will see each other really soon. I am so happy to call you my Sister, my Friend!! Much love sent your way always, miss you more. Have a spectacular birthday!!

Hugs & love

– Fran.

Notes

Notes

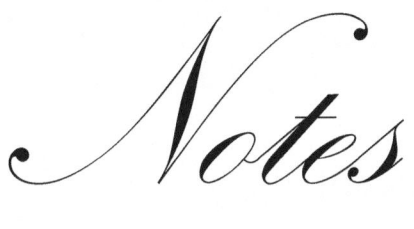

Notes

Notes